Murder
in the
Caravan

A Redmond and Haze Mystery
Book 4

By Irina Shapiro

Copyright

© 2021 by Irina Shapiro.

All rights reserved. No part of this book may be reproduced in any form, except for quotations in printed reviews, without permission in writing from the author.

All characters are fictional. Any resemblances to actual people (except those who are actual historical figures) are purely coincidental.

Chapter 23 195
Chapter 24 206
Chapter 25 215
Chapter 26 223
Chapter 27 235
Chapter 28 241
Chapter 29 251
Chapter 30 256
Chapter 31 261
Chapter 32 265
Chapter 33 270
Chapter 34 275
Chapter 35 290
Chapter 36 293
Epilogue 300
Notes..303
An Excerpt from Murder in the Grave 304
A Redmond and Haze Mystery Book 5 304
Chapter 1 307
Chapter 2 312
Chapter 3 317

Table of Contents

Copyright ....

Table of Contents...

Prologue..

Chapter 1 ....

Chapter 2 1

Chapter 3 34

Chapter 4 42

Chapter 5 57

Chapter 6 68

Chapter 7 75

Chapter 8 84

Chapter 9 97

Chapter 10 102

Chapter 11 106

Chapter 12 111

Chapter 13 117

Chapter 14 120

Chapter 15 124

Chapter 16 128

Chapter 17 134

Chapter 18 142

Chapter 19 150

Chapter 20 163

Chapter 21 168

Chapter 22 182

Prologue

Glowing rays of the morning sun sliced through the thick canopy of leaves, dappling the dewy grass with patches of sunlight. The meadow sparkled beneath a cloudless blue sky, the birds performing their arias as if for a rapt audience. Luca never tired of watching the world come to life, nor did he question the nomad lifestyle of his ancestors. Most people dreamed of living their lives tied to a piece of land, toiling endlessly and passing their woes to future generations, but Luca loved life on the road, the promise of new places, fresh sights, and unexpected loves.

He smiled broadly as he recalled last night. That had certainly been unexpected, but all the more wonderful for it. He took one last look at the sleeping woman in the bed and closed the caravan door softly behind him before cutting across the meadow toward his own caravan, all the way at the far end. Borzo came trotting toward him, pushing his wet nose into Luca's palm.

"Good morning, dog," Luca said, and patted the mutt on its head. Borzo looked all set to follow Luca to his caravan but changed his mind when Luca's mother stepped out of his parents' caravan, ready to get breakfast started. Borzo instantly turned tail and ran off.

"Traitor," Luca said under his breath before greeting his mother, who gave him a knowing look. He ignored it and skipped up the steps of his caravan. He pulled open the door, stepped inside, and nearly crashed headlong onto the floor when he tripped over something that lay in his path.

Luca grabbed the doorjamb for support and moved sideways, allowing the morning light to illuminate the dim interior. He gasped and took a step back, nearly tumbling backward down the steps. A young woman was stretched out on the floor, her face pale as marble and just as stony. Her eyes were wide open, a grimace of pain and fear etched into her lovely features. He hadn't noticed it at first, but a thin line ran across her throat, the cut so deep it must have nearly severed her head. A pool of congealed blood glistened darkly beneath the woman's head, forming a gruesome halo.

    Stumbling outside, Luca ran toward his parents' caravan. His father would know what to do.

Chapter 1

Wednesday, May 8, 1867

Jason Redmond scraped the razor across his lean cheeks and watched in the mirror as his valet, Henley, went about laying out his clothes. Henley was often bleary-eyed and pale in the mornings, given his love of strong drink, but today was different. He didn't appear hungover, just worried and sad, emotions that were completely at odds with his good-natured personality.

"Are you all right?" Jason asked as he wiped the remaining soap off his face and approached the man.

"Yes, sir."

Jason cocked his head to the side. "Are you ill?"

"No, sir. Just worried, I suppose."

"What about?" Jason asked as he picked up the shirt Henley had prepared.

"Moll Brody never came home last night," Henley said, inadvertently revealing that he'd been at the tavern until closing time.

"From where?"

"No one knows, sir. Just went out in the afternoon and never came back. Davy Brody is mad with worry," Henley said.

Jason dressed in silence, his mind on Moll Brody. He'd known her for nearly a year now, having met her when he'd first arrived in Birch Hill from New York to claim his late grandfather's estate. Moll was a fixture in Birch Hill, but Jason didn't really know anything of her life beyond the fact that she helped her uncle run the Red Stag tavern. Moll's lush beauty and sharp tongue often gave people, men in particular, the wrong idea, and she had something of a reputation in the village for being loose.

Many years ago, in medical school, a friend of Jason's had been fond of sharing his theory about women's libido with his fellow students over a pint. Chett Bleaker had said that women could be divided into three categories. The first were those who would gladly choose celibacy if it didn't have the unfortunate side effect of spinsterhood. The second, respectable women who enjoyed the attentions of their husbands but didn't display any appetites that would be considered unnatural. And the third, those rare women whose desires could match those of any man and who were the sort of women one took as lovers. Jason hadn't much liked Chett or agreed with his opinions but thought that most people would slot Moll into the third category. She was so overtly sensual, it was impossible not to feel an answering desire when confronted with such frank interest.

Despite many thinly veiled invitations, Jason had managed to resist Moll's charms, but he wondered if Moll might have found herself a fancy man and was with him right now.

"I'm sure she'll turn up," Jason said as Henley expertly tied his cravat. "Moll is clever and resourceful. Perhaps she had an argument with her uncle and decided she needed a bit of space."

Henley's eyebrows lifted in astonishment. "And gone where to get it, sir? She has no other family or friends she can stay with."

"Please inform me when she returns. I'd like to know she's safe."

"Yes, my lord," Henley replied.

Jason made his way downstairs and entered the dining room. Most mornings, he found Mr. Sullivan, his ward's tutor, already at breakfast, but this morning Jason appeared to be the first to come down.

"Morning, sir," Fanny greeted him cheerfully as she entered the dining room. "The usual?"

"Please." Jason's brain didn't operate at full capacity until he'd had at least two cups of coffee. Mrs. Dodson always sent up two fried eggs, a rasher of bacon, grilled tomato and some mushrooms with toast and butter for his breakfast, which he quite enjoyed. Jason reached for a freshly ironed newspaper that Dodson had left for him and scanned the headlines as he waited for his meal.

He had nearly finished breakfast when Dodson himself appeared, looking as exasperated as ever. He still hadn't forgiven Jason his refusal to hire proper staff and thought their unorthodox household was probably the butt of the county gossip. Jason didn't much care. Being American, he preferred to do things his own way and saw no reason to have twenty people look after the needs of four.

"Inspector Haze is here to see you," Dodson intoned, his nostrils flaring with indignation.

"Show him in here and ask Fanny to set another place," Jason said.

"There's no time for that." Daniel Haze's voice came from behind Dodson's shoulder. He sounded tense and upset.

"What's happened, Daniel? Is it Sarah?"

Sarah Haze was due to give birth any day now, and Jason had intended to be on hand during delivery should any complications arise. He'd performed a cesarean section on a village woman last autumn and had saved her and her baby from certain death, earning Sarah's complete trust. She was wary of the new doctor, whom she thought old-fashioned in his methods and unpleasant in his manner. Since she was correct on both counts, Jason was more than happy to step in.

"No, Sarah is well," Daniel replied.

"Is it Moll Brody?" Jason asked carefully.

"No. Why would you ask that?"

"Henley said Moll never came home last night. Davy is worried sick."

"And how would Henley know that?" Daniel asked.

"I can only assume he was at the Red Stag last night. Thankfully, he managed not to overindulge. But never mind that. What has happened?"

Daniel's shoulders seemed to sag under the weight of the news. "It's Imogen Chadwick, Jason," he said quietly. "She's been murdered."

"Imogen Chadwick?" Jason repeated, unable to fully accept what Daniel was telling him. "Are you certain?"

"That it's Imogen or that she's been murdered?" Daniel asked wearily.

Imogen Chadwick had recently married Harry Chadwick, one of the wealthiest men in the county, and was the daughter of Squire Talbot, who owned most of the village and ruled it as if it were a medieval fiefdom, much as his ancestors had done since the Crusades, when they had settled in these parts and claimed the land for their own. Imogen was quiet and shy, and despite her typical English prettiness was the type of young woman people tended to overlook on account of her demure disposition. Having to now share a house with her widowed mother-in-law, Caroline Chadwick, a woman one should only cross at one's own risk, and her two sisters-in-law, Arabella and Lucinda, Imogen couldn't have been having an easy time of it after being sheltered and doted on by her parents. They'd arranged the marriage to their closest neighbor long before Imogen was at the age of consent in the hopes of binding the two houses in a union of material bliss, made even sweeter by the combined social power the two families wielded in the county.

The very notion that someone would wish to harm Imogen seemed utterly preposterous and unexpectedly personal. Jason had assisted Inspector Haze and the Brentwood Constabulary on several cases, but this was the first time he'd known the victim.

"I'm afraid so, on both counts. I need you to accompany me, Jason. Examine the body. I left Constable Pullman to keep watch."

Jason pushed away his plate and stood, shoving the chair back so hard it scraped against the floor.

Dodson was already in the foyer, Jason's coat, hat, and gloves at the ready. Fanny, who must have overheard the conversation and hurried upstairs to fetch Jason's medical bag, held it out to him, her gaze filled with anxiety. Jason didn't think he'd be needing any medical supplies, given that Imogen was beyond his help, but he thanked Fanny for her thoughtfulness and followed Daniel out the door.

"I brought the dogcart," Daniel said as they stepped into the glorious May morning. "It's quite a ways."

"Where exactly was she found?"

"At the encampment. One of the Travelers tripped over her this morning."

"Can you kindly translate that?" Jason asked.

"Sorry. You wouldn't know what I mean, of course. Every year, around this time, Romani Gypsies set up camp in Bloody Mead. Imogen was found in one of their caravans."

"Bloody Mead? Did someone die there after overindulging in tainted mead?" Jason asked. The English had a creative if somewhat peculiar way of naming things, and he quite enjoyed learning the history behind the monikers, since the names usually went back generations and were always meaningful to those who'd lived in the area.

"It's named after a wildflower, actually," Daniel replied. "Bloody Cranesbill, or some such. It's quite pretty. When it blooms, it's like a purple quilt spread over the meadow. Mead is short for meadow," he added.

"What would Imogen Chadwick have been doing in a Gypsy caravan?" Jason asked.

"That's what I mean to find out," Daniel replied as he guided the horse down a narrow track through the woods.

"So, are you here as Inspector Haze of the Brentwood Constabulary or as the former Birch Hill parish constable? I was under the impression that all legal matters pertaining to the village fell to Squire Talbot."

"Bloody Mead lies outside the parameters of Birch Hill, so Squire Talbot has no legal jurisdiction over the Romani, and given that the victim is his daughter, it's best for everyone if the investigation is handled by a professional police force."

"Has Squire Talbot been informed?" Jason asked.

"Not yet. Detective Inspector Coleridge wanted us to confirm the identity of the victim and examine the body before informing the next of kin."

"Who reported the crime?" Jason asked.

"The Romani sent a boy to the station."

"That's very civic minded of them," Jason observed.

Daniel shrugged. "Normally, the Romani avoid the police like the proverbial plague, since the law is rarely on their side, but in this instance, they probably decided that it was in their best interests to get ahead of this situation."

"I don't see how this will help them," Jason said. "Reporting a body found in one of their caravans is practically admitting that one of their own is responsible."

Daniel shrugged. "I won't argue with you there, but had they decided to dispose of the body, the investigation would focus on them anyway, seeing as they are strangers and are always treated with suspicion and resentment, and such an action would only convince the police they have something to hide. Ah, we're nearly there."

Chapter 2

Jason looked ahead, his mouth opening in surprise when the trees parted and Bloody Mead, liberally dotted with the flower it was named after, came into view. He'd never seen a Gypsy camp before, and the sight came as something of a surprise. He supposed he'd expected a handful of makeshift tents and rickety wagons, but what he saw had an almost magical quality. There were about ten caravans grouped around the meadow, the bright exteriors embellished with beautiful designs that had been skillfully painted. Each dwelling was a work of art, unique in color and design.

Several people were about. The men sat around, talking quietly, while the women, who were dressed in colorful skirts and wore gold jewelry, tended their cooking fires and kept an eye on the children, who ran around barefoot and shouted to each other in a language Jason didn't understand. Several horses grazed in the meadow, the breed unfamiliar to Jason. They were smaller and stockier than the horses he was used to and were black and white in coloring, almost like cows. Long fringes covered the bottom of their legs, the feathery hair blowing in the breeze.

A bulky wooden police wagon stood beneath the trees, the horse munching lazily on the grass. Ned Hollingsworth, a crime scene photographer recently hired by the commissioner of the Brentwood Police Constabulary, stood leaning against the wagon, his camera and tripod on the ground next to him where he could keep an eye on them. He lifted a hand in greeting but made no move to approach the dogcart. Having finished what he'd come to do, he was clearly ready to leave but needed a ride back into town. Ned was a taciturn man who didn't mix with the coppers, but unlike his predecessor, who had sold copies of the photographs to the newspapers, Ned was trustworthy and efficient. He would have the photographs ready by the end of the day, but for now, all Daniel Haze had to work with was the actual crime scene and his own instincts and observations.

The two men alighted from the dogcart and were approached by an older man, who appeared to be the leader. He wore a white linen shirt and wide black trousers paired with a colorful waistcoat and a red kerchief tied around his neck.

"Good morning," Daniel said politely. "I am Inspector Haze of the Brentwood Constabulary, and this is Lord Redmond, our police surgeon."

The man nodded, his expression grave and his shoulders stooped in defeat. Most people were astounded that a nobleman would act as a police surgeon, but the man didn't seem to care, clearly having more important matters on his mind.

"We mean to cooperate with the police," he said hoarsely. "We hope you keep that in mind, Inspector."

"May I know your name?" Daniel asked.

The man hesitated. "My name is Bogdan."

"Is that a surname?"

"No, it's my given name. We're not much used to using surnames."

"Do you have one?" Daniel persisted.

"Lee. It's Bogdan Lee."

"Thank you, Mr. Lee. I will need to interview everyone at the camp. Please inform them of my intention. Where is Constable Pullman?" Daniel asked, looking around for the burly policeman who was nowhere to be seen.

Bogdan gestured toward a green-painted caravan parked at the edge of the meadow. "Your man is inside with the body. He prefers the company of the dead to us," the man said with obvious bitterness.

Daniel ignored the comment. "Shall we?" he said to Jason.

Jason and Daniel approached the caravan but stopped before going in, taking time to examine the scene. Unlike the other caravans, whose doors were turned toward the center of the meadow, the green caravan was partially turned away, the door facing outward toward the surrounding forest.

"What do you think?" Jason asked after several moments.

"There is no sign of a struggle, and the door doesn't seem to have been forced. There are also no footprints, since the caravan is parked on the grass."

"The grass hasn't been flattened, which means the body wasn't dragged here."

"My thoughts exactly." Daniel walked up the wooden steps and opened the door. Jason followed. Inside, the caravan was as lovely as it was from the outside. It was painted in fanciful patterns and decorated with rich fabrics and colored glass baubles. Every space appeared to serve its own purpose and was well organized.

Constable Pullman sat on a velvet-covered bench, his shoulders stooped, his helmet in his hands. Sweat glistened on his brow even though the interior of the caravan was pleasantly cool. Constable Pullman breathed a sigh of relief when he saw Daniel.

"Thank the Lord you're here, Inspector," he said. "I was beginning to think I'd be keeping her company all day. 'Tis a gruesome sight, this is."

"You can step outside now, Constable," Daniel said. With the body on the floor, there was hardly any space for the men to stand, especially if the constable remained inside the caravan.

Constable Pullman sprang to his feet, sidestepped the body, and stepped outside, sucking in the fresh air with as much gratitude as if he'd been trapped underwater. "I'll just be by the police wagon," he said, and trotted off.

"Should I wait outside while you examine the body?" Daniel asked.

"It is rather a tight squeeze," Jason said. "You can watch through the door."

Jason positioned himself next to the body, which lay on the floor between the bench Constable Pullman had just vacated and a round-bellied stove whose pipe extended through an opening in the

15

roof. The gold-tasseled curtains were drawn, but the interior was still light enough to see an ornate bed built into the rear wall of the wagon, several cabinets, and a polished table draped with a damask cloth of pale blue. There was a jug of fresh flowers, a violin in a battered case that lay atop one of the cabinets, and several plates and cups arranged neatly on built-in shelves. The ceiling was low and curved, making Jason feel uncomfortably boxed in. He pulled open the curtains, allowing the morning light to shine onto the young woman at his feet.

Imogen lay on her back, her blue eyes bulging slightly, her mouth open as if in a silent scream. A deep, razor-thin gash encircled her throat, and there were livid scratches on both sides of her neck. Her face was cold to the touch, and her limbs had already begun to stiffen, rigor mortis having set in. Jason examined the front and back of the body, then inspected each hand in turn. All fingers except the thumbs were cut to the bone, the incision even and of the same width as the wound on her neck. Jason peered beneath the fingernails before moving on to a more intimate examination. Daniel stood on the top step of the caravan, blocking the entrance, so that Jason had complete privacy and Imogen's remains weren't exposed to idle curiosity from the Travelers who were watching the wagon in rapt silence. Daniel looked away respectfully as Jason pushed Imogen's thighs apart to examine her more closely.

Having known Imogen, Jason felt a trifle guilty for taking such liberties with her person. She would have been mortified by the intrusion and would have most likely refused such an intimate examination had she survived the attack. Jason rearranged the skirts to cover her most private areas and moved downward, focusing on the calves and ankles, then the feet, still clad in silk stockings and dainty kid slippers.

"Well?" Daniel asked at last.

Jason got to his feet and leaned against one of the cabinets, wishing he could leave the confined space and step outside into the fresh air, but they needed to speak privately, and there were too many people hovering nearby.

"Has she been violated?" Daniel asked. He looked angry and tense, and deeply embarrassed at having witnessed Jason's thorough examination of the body.

"No. There are no signs of rape. Her underclothes were not in disarray, nor are there any obvious wounds save the ones on her neck and hands. I think she came to the encampment of her own volition and entered the caravan willingly, but she did fight for her life. Her nails are torn, and there's blood and tissue beneath them—her own, I presume. She tried to insert her fingers beneath the garrote, hence the scratches on her neck, and it nearly sliced her fingers off. The killer nearly decapitated her, possibly because he or she used a thin wire that sliced through skin and muscle."

"You're sure she was garroted with a wire?" Daniel asked.

"I am. The diameter of the cut is too thin for it to have been anything else."

"When was she killed?"

"I can't give you a precise time, but based on the level of rigor, I'd say she was killed yesterday evening. She's lain here all night."

"How is that possible?" Daniel demanded. "You'd have to climb over her to get to the bed. Did no one sleep here last night?" Daniel shook his head in dismay. "Do you think the Chadwicks will agree to a postmortem?"

"I seriously doubt that," Jason replied. "Nor do I think it will tell us much more than we already know. The cause of death is obvious."

Imogen had been young and healthy, and seemed to have suffered no internal injuries. Jason had palpated her belly but couldn't tell if she might have been pregnant. At this stage, he wouldn't be able to know for certain without dissecting the womb. Normally, he would advocate for a postmortem, but he saw no reason to cut Imogen Chadwick up. Or perhaps it was his own reluctance to perform an autopsy on someone he'd known personally.

"Let's get the body in the wagon, and I'll have Constable Pullman take it to the station. The Chadwicks can collect the remains once we're ready to release the body. Once Pullman is off, I'm going to start interviewing the suspects," Daniel said.

"Are they all suspects, then?"

"I have to work under the assumption that they are until I can rule some of them out, which might prove difficult, as the Romani are not known for being truthful or straightforward, not that I can blame them. People are generally not well disposed toward them."

Jason stepped out of the caravan, relieved to be in the open air. No matter how beautifully appointed, the small space made him anxious. He returned his unopened medical bag to the dogcart, while Constable Pullman and Daniel carried Imogen Chadwick's remains to the police wagon and arranged the body inside. His only contact with the dead through the lens of his camera, Ned Hollingsworth made no effort to help and climbed onto the bench, ready to leave as soon as Constable Pullman was ready to go. The constable looked like a man sprung from jail as he pulled away, eager to be away from the campsite where he'd spent the past few hours with only a dead woman for company.

The Gypsy tribe was gathered in the meadow, most people silent and watchful as Jason and Daniel approached. There were eleven men, eight women, and at least a dozen children of varying ages, whose expressions ranged from open-mouthed curiosity to obvious hostility.

Daniel addressed Bogdan, who came toward him. "May I use one of your caravans to conduct the interviews?" he asked.

"You can use mine," Bogdan said. "It's the red one." He pointed to one of the larger caravans. "Would you care for tea?"

Daniel seemed taken aback by this gesture of hospitality but instantly rearranged his features. "Yes, thank you. That's very kind."

Bogdan gestured to an older woman who had to be his wife, and she nodded in acknowledgement. "I will bring it inside," she said.

"I'd like to speak to the person who found the body first," Daniel said.

"Would you like me to be present during the interviews or wait out here?" Jason asked.

"Please, come inside. I would appreciate your point of view in this matter," Daniel replied, holding the door open for Jason.

Reluctantly, Jason entered the caravan and settled on a bench beneath the window. Thankfully, this wagon was a bit wider, and the windows on both sides made it feel less coffin-like.

A swarthy young man appeared in the doorway, his dark gaze defiant. "I found her, Inspector."

Daniel gestured for him to step into the caravan and take a seat at the round table. "Name?"

"Luca."

"Surname?" Daniel asked.

"Lee. Bogdan Lee is my father," the young man said. He couldn't be more than twenty-two, and although he wasn't traditionally good-looking, there was something charming about his youthful face.

"Please, tell me what happened, Mr. Lee," Daniel invited.

Luca closed his eyes for a moment, as if trying to visualize what he'd seen, then began to speak, his voice low and melodious. "I returned to my vardo just as the sun came up. Vardo is a caravan," he clarified. "The curtains were drawn, so it was dark inside, and I nearly tripped over her. At first, I thought she'd fallen asleep, but when I shifted away from the door and the light fell on her face, I knew she was dead."

"What did you do?"

"I roused my father and told him what had happened. He sent one of the boys to fetch the police."

"You did not sleep in your caravan last night?" Daniel asked.

"No, I spent the night with a friend," the young man said, a sly smile spreading across his face. He didn't need to clarify that his friend was a woman.

"Do you live in the caravan alone?" Jason asked.

"For now."

"What does that mean?" Daniel inquired.

"I hope to be married soon, then I'll share the caravan with my wife," Luca explained.

"And when did you leave your caravan yesterday?" Daniel asked, watching the young man intently.

"Just before breakfast."

"So, it had been left empty for approximately twenty-four hours?" Jason asked.

"That's right."

"Where did you go?" Jason asked.

"Some lads and I had business to attend to," Luca replied, his gaze sliding away and fixing on the ornate bed carvings.

"What sort of business?" Daniel asked.

"We went to look at some horses we considered buying," Luca replied. He looked too shifty for Daniel to believe him, but Daniel made no comment. He wasn't here about horses, either bought or stolen.

"Did you know the deceased?" Daniel asked instead.

"Not to talk to, but I've seen her around."

"Have you, indeed?" Daniel asked, pinning Luca with his gaze.

"Look, Inspector, I was born in this meadow and have come back every year since. We don't have much to do with the villagers, but we do know them by sight, and I have seen that one before. Last summer."

"She came to the camp?" Daniel and Jason asked nearly in unison.

Luca nodded. "You need to speak to Zamfira. She'll be able to tell you more. She does some *dukkerin* for the *gorjas*."

"I beg your pardon?" Jason said, his face a mask of incomprehension.

"Fortune telling for the locals," Luca explained.

"Can you send her in, please?" Daniel said, making a note in his little notebook.

"Are we done here?" Luca asked.

"For now."

Luca left the caravan, and a young woman stepped inside. She was one of the most beautiful women Daniel had ever seen. With riotous dark curls, eyes the color of black coffee, and full, rosy lips, she looked foreign, and her colorful clothing and dangly gold jewelry made her appear even more exotic. Daniel cleared his throat and consulted his notebook, needing a moment to compose himself. He had a heavily pregnant wife at home; he had no business admiring other women's beauty, even if the observation had been dispassionate.

"Eh, name please," Daniel said, his pencil suspended over a clean page.

"Zamfira Lee," the young woman replied.

"Are you Luca's sister?"

"Sister-in-law," Zamfira corrected him.

"Did you know the deceased?" Daniel asked, studying her through the lenses of his spectacles, which magnified her already huge eyes.

"Yes. She came to the encampment last year. To have her fortune told."

"And she came to have her fortune told yesterday?"

"She did."

"Did you charge her?" Daniel asked.

"Of course. Why wouldn't I?" Zamfira asked, clearly surprised by the question.

"Did you tell her she was about to die?" Daniel asked, immediately ashamed of the sarcasm in his voice. "Did you see it?"

"I saw she wasn't long for this world, Inspector, but I had no way of knowing she'd die just after she left me. And no, I didn't tell her."

"So, what did you say to her?" Jason asked, curious how Zamfira handled dire predictions.

"I told her she'd live a long and happy life," Zamfira said smugly, her eyes flashing with amusement.

"Is that what you tell all the gullible young women who come to see you?" Daniel demanded.

"No, not all, but seeing as she wasn't going to be around long enough to disprove what I told her, I thought I'd let her die happy."

"What time did she come to see you?" Daniel asked.

Zamfira shrugged. "I don't own a watch, but if I had to guess, I'd say close to four. Maybe a bit later."

"And what did she do after the reading? Did she speak to anyone else?"

Zamfira made a show of thinking. "No, she silvered my palm, thanked me, and walked away."

"And what did you do after she left?" Jason asked.

"I went inside to nurse my baby," Zamfira replied. "Once I got him to sleep, I came back out to help my mother-in-law with supper."

"So, you didn't see Imogen Chadwick enter Luca's caravan?" Daniel asked, his gaze fixed on the young woman before him.

"No, I didn't."

"Thank you. That will be all," Daniel said. He sighed and called for the next person to enter.

Two hours later, Daniel and Jason finally emerged from the caravan. Daniel had a massive headache, and Jason looked like he was about to be sick.

"I don't like closed spaces," Jason said, breathing deeply as he walked toward the dogcart, the greenish tint fading from his skin and normal color reasserting itself.

"You should have said," Daniel replied, and climbed onto the bench, taking up the reins.

Jason gave a dismissive wave, his expression thoughtful as he settled next to Daniel. The Romani had kindly fed and watered the horse while he interviewed everyone in the tribe.

"So, what do you think?" Daniel asked. "Sounds like they'd all rehearsed their story before we got here."

"Either they rehearsed it or it's true. Have they ever murdered anyone that you know of?" Jason asked.

"Not murdered, as such, but there have been thefts, numerous incidents of illness, and general bad luck."

"And you think they're responsible?" Jason asked, clearly incredulous.

"I really couldn't say. I try to keep an open mind, but given that none of them have steady employment and spend their lives gallivanting from place to place, you have to wonder where their income comes from. How much can you make telling fortunes and selling baskets in the market? No doubt you've noticed how richly the caravans are decorated and what good horses they have. Finery doesn't come cheap."

"No, I don't suppose it does," Jason said, but he didn't sound convinced. "Where to now?"

Daniel sighed heavily. "Before we do anything, we must inform the next of kin."

Jason tilted his head to the side, a speculative gleam in his eyes. "Daniel, does it not strike you as odd that Imogen Chadwick has been deceased since yesterday evening, possibly late afternoon, and no one has reported her missing? Surely the Chadwicks would have noticed she wasn't at dinner."

"Perhaps not," Daniel replied. "I can't imagine she'd have told anyone she was coming to the Gypsy encampment. Perhaps she pled a headache, or some other illness, and everyone just assumed she'd retired early. Many married couples don't share a bed, so it's quite possible no one has realized she's not in her room." Daniel pulled out his pocket watch and consulted it. "It's nearly eleven. I wager the family is just now starting to suspect that something is wrong." He exhaled loudly. "Perhaps it's best if you don't come with me," he said. "Having you there will lead to awkward questions about the examination of the body."

"Drop me off at the gate. I'll walk home."

"Perhaps you can do me a favor," Daniel said, wishing with all his might that he didn't have to be the one to relay the heartbreaking news to the family. "Stop in at the Red Stag and see if Moll's come back."

"Do you think Moll's disappearance is relevant to the murder?" Jason asked.

"Don't you?"

"I suppose it's possible," Jason conceded.

"And speak to Matty Locke. Very little gets past that boy. Maybe he noticed something unusual."

"Like what?"

"Like a stranger arriving in the village," Daniel suggested. Given the nature of village life, anyone who wasn't a local would immediately become a suspect.

"Of course," Jason agreed, but he seemed distracted. "I'm curious about the dog."

"What?"

"I saw a dog. There might be more than one. Would they not have barked if a stranger had walked into the camp?" Jason asked. "Besides, what reason would a passing stranger have to kill Imogen Chadwick, and why on earth would he do it in a Gypsy caravan?"

Daniel shook his head, mystified by the whole business. "I honestly have no idea, Jason. No idea at all."

Chapter 3

The Red Stag was virtually empty except for a few regulars who were nursing their tankards despite the early hour. Dust motes danced in the shafts of light coming from the mullioned windows, and the smell of spilled alcohol permeated the air. Davy Brody stood behind the bar, his expression vacant. He always reminded Jason of a pugilist who was about to enter the ring, but today he looked as if he'd already been defeated, the match lost. Jason walked up to the bar.

"Good day, Mr. Brody," Jason said. The man inclined his head in acknowledgement.

"Has Moll come home?" Jason asked without preamble. There seemed little sense in beating about the bush.

"She has not. What's it to ye, yer lordship?"

"A young woman was found dead this morning," Jason began, and instantly regretted his thoughtless words.

Davy paled as his mouth opened in shock. "Is it…?"

"No. No," Jason hurried to reassure him. "It's not Moll, but given what happened, Inspector Haze is concerned for Moll's well-being."

"She's not 'ere," Davy said hoarsely. "She went out round three yesterday afternoon and never came back."

"Where did she go?"

"Said she needed some air," Davy replied. "Went for a walk." Davy averted his gaze, focusing it on the mug he was wiping.

"Where does she normally walk?" Jason inquired.

Davy shrugged. "I don't know."

"Did you look for her?"

Davy shook his head. "Full 'ouse last night. Couldn't leave the premises." Davy set the empty mug down with a hollow thud and glared at Jason. "I'll organize a search party. We'll find 'er."

"I think that's an excellent idea. No doubt Roger Henley will wish to help."

"I'd rather 'e didn't," Davy growled. "Always sniffing around 'er like she were a bitch in 'eat. She's a good girl, Moll. No matter what ye lot think."

"I have the utmost respect for Moll," Jason replied. That wasn't strictly true, given that Moll had brazenly offered herself to him on several occasions, but he did like her and hoped she was safe.

"Moll's my only family," Davy said softly, his gaze sorrowful. "I do care for 'er," he added.

"Of course," Jason replied. "Please send word to Constable Haze if you find Moll." *Alive or dead*, Jason added inwardly.

"Who was the lass that died?" Davy asked.

"I'm not at liberty to say," Jason replied. The news would reach the Red Stag soon enough.

"Can ye tell me 'ow she died, at least?" Davy persisted.

"She was garroted."

"Where?"

"In one of the Gypsy caravans."

"Lord 'ave mercy on 'er soul," Davy exclaimed. "Did she suffer, guv?"

"It would have been quick," Jason lied. Imogen would have known what was happening, would have had time to feel panic, and terror, and pain, but he saw no reason to share that with the publican, not when his niece might have suffered the same fate.

"Did Moll ever visit the Gypsy campsite?" Jason asked. He thought Davy would be surprised or even outraged by the question, but he seemed to draw in on himself, pulling his head in like a turtle.

27

"She always went to see them, as soon as they came," Davy said morosely. "She were drawn to them."

"Why?" Jason prompted.

Davy looked away, fixing his stare on St. Catherine's Church through the front window, its solid shape distorted by the wavy panes. Davy seemed to be wrestling with indecision. Then he suddenly slapped his hands on the bar and nodded, as if he'd come to some inevitable conclusion. "Come with me," Davy said, beckoning to Jason to follow him to the small office behind the bar, where he kept his more valuable stock and tavern ledgers. He gestured toward the rickety cane chair he kept for visitors and sat down behind the desk, practically falling into the seat, which creaked ominously beneath his bulk. Jason remained silent, waiting for Davy to speak.

"I may as well tell ye, given what's happened, but I'll 'ave yer word as a gentleman that this goes no further than Inspector Haze." He stared at Jason belligerently, daring him to refuse.

"You have my word, Mr. Brody," Jason said, wondering what on earth Davy was about to impart.

Davy exhaled loudly and stared at his splayed hands for a moment, as if still unsure if he should speak. This was obviously difficult for him, and he would no doubt regret what he was about to share, but his affection for Moll finally won out.

"My sister, Rachel, took up with one of the Travelers when she were fifteen. 'E were a fine-looking cove, turned 'er silly 'ead with words of love and little trinkets 'e lifted from honest folk. My father, 'e put an end to it right quick when 'e found out, but not before she got with child. Now, my father, 'e were an 'ard man, but 'e loved 'is Rachel. Couldn't bear to see 'er earning 'er keep as a dollymop."

"Sorry?" Jason interjected, unfamiliar with the term.

"A whore," Davy clarified angrily. "'Ave ye never been to a dollyshop, man?"

Jason didn't reply. "Please, go on," he said instead.

"My father put the word out that Rachel were to wed one of the farm 'ands, and she would 'ave, but the man done a runner before the banns were called. Didn't appreciate being my father's tool. My father, oh 'e were angry, but 'e'd done what 'e set out to do. Made everyone think the scoundrel got Rachel with child and run out on 'er. There was still talk, mind ye, but Rachel was young and sweet, and soon enough the gossip died down. Rachel, she doted on Moll. Loved the life out of that girl, 'cause she loved the father, ye see. Never got over losing 'im," Davy said sadly.

"What happened to Rachel?" Jason asked softly.

"Rachel died when Moll were seven. Our parents weren't far behind. So I sold the farm, bought this place, and took Moll in. Some might say different, but I love 'er in my own way."

"I've no doubt you do," Jason said.

"Ye know what it's like to love a child that ain't yers," Davy said, nodding his understanding. "I seen the way ye look at that Irish lad. 'E's the son ye never 'ad."

"Micah and I have a stronger bond than many fathers and sons," Jason agreed. He had no wish to elaborate. What he shared with Micah was private and had nothing to do with the case. "Did Moll know who her father was?"

"I never told 'er, and she never asked."

"Do you know his name?" Jason asked, wondering if Moll's father had been of the same tribe as the one camped out in Bloody Mead.

"Andrei Lee." Davy spat out the name as if it were something foul.

"And did this Andrei Lee know Moll was his daughter?"

"Aye, 'e did. Came for 'er after Rachel died. Said 'e'd cared for Rachel and would be glad to be a father to 'is girl, if we'd let 'im. My father chased 'im off. Nearly shot the poor bastard's 'ead off."

"Do you think any of the Lees told Moll she was a relation?" Jason asked, still trying to absorb the fact that Moll was half-Romani. He hadn't expected that.

Davy shook his head. "Moll never said nothin', and I think she would 'ave had a lot to say 'ad she found out. She's not one to keep 'er feelings to 'erself, if ye know what I mean. They was always kind to 'er, though," he added. "Made 'er feel welcome. Well, I best be getting on. I 'ave a search party to round up."

Jason nodded. "I hope you find her, safe and sound."

Having left the Red Stag, Jason walked a few paces to the stable yard, where Matty Locke was filling a trough with water.

The boy smiled in welcome. "Hello, guv."

"Hello, Matty," Jason said. "How's the leg?" Matty had broken his leg a few months back, but there was no sign of the injury now.

"Right as rain, yer lordship. I can't thank ye enough for looking after me," Matty said. "Is there aught I can 'elp ye with?"

"Matty, have you seen any strangers in the village over the past few days?" Jason asked.

Matty looked heavenward as he considered the question. "Well, I don't know if they's strangers, exactly."

"Whom did you see?" Jason asked, eager to get Matty talking.

"Well, the Gypsies, of course. They came 'bout three days since, but they do every summer," he said.

"Anyone else?"

"Sir Lawrence arrived on Sunday afternoon."

"Sir Lawrence?" Jason asked, trying to recall where he'd heard the name before.

Matty nodded enthusiastically. "Sir Lawrence Foxley. 'E 'as a fine carriage," Matty said dreamily. "And a lovely pair of grays."

"Where is he staying, Matty?" Jason asked, hoping to focus the boy's attention on the matter at hand.

"Chadwick 'All, of course, seeing as 'ow 'e's Miss Lucinda's intended."

Now the name fell into place. He'd heard Lucinda Chadwick was betrothed, and given the number of times her mother had uttered the words "Sir Lawrence Foxley, Baronet" within hearing distance, he should have remembered.

"Did Sir Lawrence come alone?" Jason asked.

"Well, 'e 'ad 'is coachman, of course, and 'is valet," Matty replied, giving Jason a look of bafflement that said that being a nobleman himself, Jason should know better than to ask such a foolish question.

"Right. Thank you, Matty." Jason tossed Matty a coin, which the boy deftly caught, and headed toward the vicarage, cutting across the village green.

31

Chapter 4

Despite the sad circumstances, Jason was glad to have an excuse to call on Katherine. They had been engaged for nearly five months, but her father, Reverend Talbot, still made it difficult for them to meet, insisting that Katherine must not spend time with Jason unchaperoned and accompanying her to Redmond Hall whenever Katherine paid a social call. Jason supposed the reverend was just trying to protect his daughter from village gossip, or perhaps he didn't trust Jason to go through with the wedding. He'd heard of instances where a wealthy, titled young man would stage a fake wedding in order to bed a woman he desired and then leave her as soon as he tired of her, informing her their marriage wasn't valid and he owed her nothing. Few women thus treated were able to recover their good name or position in society, even though they were the victim and not the perpetrator.

Had it been up to Jason, he and Katherine would be married already, but the reverend had insisted on a betrothal of six months. Reverend Talbot was a selfish, pedantic man who felt it was Katherine's duty to look after him and his parishioners in lieu of his wife, who was long gone, rather than see to her own happiness. Jason also strongly suspected that despite the Redmond wealth and title, there were elements that put the reverend on guard, or more accurately, set his teeth on edge. Since Jason was American by birth, the reverend viewed him as a lawless barbarian who was ignorant of the ways of society, had no honor, and acted in a way unbecoming to his station. Jason only reinforced this belief when he agreed to act as an on-call police surgeon for the Brentwood Constabulary, a sideline that gave Jason purpose and allowed him to practice his surgical skills.

Jason was also legal guardian to Micah Donavan, an Irish orphan he'd informally adopted after Micah's father and brother had died during their incarceration at Andersonville Prison, where Jason had also been held during the final year of the American Civil War. A few months ago, Jason had opened his home to Micah's sister Mary and her infant son Liam, whose illegitimate status was known only to Jason and Mary herself. Throw in a

Catholic, homosexual tutor and a boozer of a valet who often carried messages between Katherine and Jason instead of seeing to Jason's sadly unimpressive wardrobe, and Redmond Hall was synonymous with a den of iniquity, of which the reverend's daughter would soon be mistress.

The reverend was of the opinion that Micah, heathen though he was, should be sent to school in short order, and a nanny should be engaged for Liam so that the little boy could stop hurtling himself down the extensive corridors of the hall and become silent and invisible, as a child should be. Reverend Talbot had never got the chance to express his views on Mary's situation or Shawn Sullivan's proclivities, since Jason had politely asked him to leave before he gave in to the impulse to wring the reverend's neck and display it on a spike by the gate to ward off any other well-meaning sycophants who had an opinion on the respectability of Jason's household.

Thankfully, Katherine was a young woman of great intelligence and strong opinions and would not be swayed from her decision to marry "that American degenerate," as her father had once referred to Jason within his hearing. Her loyalty and need to defend him endeared her to Jason even more, and he thanked his lucky stars that he'd managed to win her love.

"Jason," Katherine exclaimed when she opened the door of the vicarage. "What a pleasant surprise. I'm afraid I can't invite you in," she said, making a face. "Father is not at home to chaperone us."

"Perhaps we can allow God to chaperone us instead," Jason replied, ignoring Katherine's raised eyebrows. "Surely he wouldn't object to us speaking in church."

Katherine thought about that for a moment. "No, I suppose not. Although, degenerate that you are, I wouldn't expect you to keep your hands to yourself, even in the house of the Lord."

Jason held out his hand to her. "Come, walk with me."

"I can't go out like this," Katherine exclaimed, giving him a look of exasperation. "One second. I need to put on my bonnet and fetch my gloves." She returned a moment later, ready to go, and they strolled toward the church, passing through the peaceful graveyard, with its ancient yews and weather-worn headstones.

The church was pleasantly cool and conveniently empty. Katherine and Jason took one of the back pews and turned to face each other, drinking each other in as if they hadn't seen each other in weeks, when in fact it had only been two days.

Katherine reached up and touched his face, her eyes aglow with love. "Soon, my love," she said. "Only a few more weeks, and father will have no power over us. I've been reading up on Florence," she added, having been preparing for their wedding trip as only Katherine would. "Oh, Jason, there's so much to see."

Jason took her hand and brought it to his lips. "I, for one, can't wait. The thought of our honeymoon is the only thing that keeps me going," he confessed.

Katherine blushed to the roots of her hair and gave him a reproachful look.

"Can a man not look forward to visiting art museums and endless churches in his quest for enlightenment?" Jason quipped, and instantly fell silent, deeply aware of the impropriety of making jokes while an innocent young woman lay in the mortuary, her head having been nearly severed from her neck.

"I never realized you were so fond of art," Katherine said. "What is it?" she asked, aware of the change in Jason's demeanor. "Has something happened? Is it Moll? I heard she never came home last night."

Jason braced himself. Imogen had not only been Katherine's friend, she was her cousin. They'd known each other since birth and had shared many happy hours together, especially while Katherine's mother and sister had been alive and Kathrine had often been taken to Squire Talbot's sprawling manor house for tea and to play in the garden while the women visited with each other.

"Moll is still missing, but there's something else, Katie. Imogen Chadwick has been murdered. Her body was found in a Gypsy caravan this morning."

Katherine's hand flew to her mouth. "No!" she exclaimed. "No." Her eyes filled with tears, and her shoulders sagged as if Jason had suddenly draped them in a mantle too heavy for her slight frame. He reached out and took her hand, and she clasped her fingers around his, squeezing tightly enough to make him wince.

"Oh, Jason, why would anyone want to kill Imogen? She was so good, so kind. Do you think the Travelers killed her?" she asked, watching his face for any hint of information he was keeping from her.

"I don't know, Katie. The evidence certainly points in that direction. It stands to reason that she had gone to the caravan to meet someone or had been lured inside by someone who meant her harm."

"Why would she go to the Gypsy camp?" Katherine asked. She was frowning, trying to make sense of what he was telling her.

"She liked to have her fortune told," Jason replied. "She'd been there before, or so the Travelers would have us believe. Have you ever had your fortune told?" He couldn't see Imogen going to the campsite by herself. By all accounts, she had been shy and reticent. She would have needed someone to come with her.

Katherine let go of his hand, and not a moment too soon. Jason was beginning to lose feeling in his fingers. He flexed them to get the circulation going but kept his gaze on Katherine.

She sighed and glanced toward the altar, her expression one of all-encompassing guilt. "I have. Father had forbidden us to go. He said it was heathen, and God would punish us for seeking to discover something that was only for Him to know."

"But you went anyway," Jason said softly.

Katherine nodded. "Once."

"Did you go with Imogen?"

"No. Anne and I went. After Anne died, some part of me thought that God had taken my sister as punishment for disobeying our father." Katherine exhaled loudly.

"Surely you no longer believe that," Jason said, wishing he could lighten her burden.

"No. Anne had consumption. I know it wasn't my fault, but I suppose it was easier to blame myself than to think her death was random."

"I'm sorry. I know you miss her," Jason said.

Katherine nodded, but the sorrow in her gaze had already been replaced with determination. "How can I help? You must let me help," she said, turning to face him.

"You can share everything you know with me," Jason replied.

"But I don't know anything. How could I?"

"You may have seen or heard something. Katie, have you met Sir Lawrence?" Jason asked.

Katherine's delicate eyebrows lifted in surprise. "No. Why? Do you think he had something to do with Imogen's death?"

"I have no reason to think that, but he was the only person to arrive in the village just before the murder, aside from the Gypsies."

"How do you know that?"

"Matty Locke saw him. The coachman had stopped to ask for directions to Chadwick Manor."

"I've never met the man, but I've certainly heard a lot about him," Katherine said.

"Tell me everything," Jason invited.

Katherine's eyebrows knitted in concentration as she tried to recall the details. "Father and I have been to Chadwick Manor several times since the family returned from London in March. They came back for Christmas, but if I remember correctly, Lucinda only met Sir Lawrence in January. It was at a ball or musical evening," Katherine said, making a dismissive gesture with her hand. "By all accounts, it was a whirlwind courtship, and Sir Lawrence proposed on St. Valentine's Day. All very romantic.

We heard the whole story when we came to tea shortly after the betrothal had been announced in the papers."

"Did Lucinda tell you about it?" Jason asked.

"No. Caroline did."

"Katie, as you know, I'm not well versed in the rules that govern the ton, but I was under the impression that the older daughter was meant to marry first," Jason said, wondering if he'd invented that bit of archaic nonsense based on what he'd heard or read in the papers.

Katherine nodded. "That would have been the case had Arabella's engagement not been called off."

"Arabella was engaged?" Jason asked. He really should pay more attention to gossip, he decided.

Katherine looked conflicted. She didn't like to tell tales, especially when they weren't about her, but this was a murder investigation, and any small detail could be relevant. "I don't know if any of this is true, mind you, so don't go repeating it," she warned him. "Well, you can tell Inspector Haze, of course, since it might have bearing on the investigation, but I really don't see how. When I went for a walk with Lucinda shortly after the family returned to Birch Hill, she intimated that Arabella's engagement had been a sham."

"In what way?"

"It seems that Lucinda had set her sights on Sir Lawrence from the very start of the Season. Being a baronet, he's an extremely desirable match for a girl who doesn't come from a noble lineage. There are those who'd call her an upstart for trying to marry up, but Lucinda is not much troubled by sentiment, not as long as she gets what she wants, and her sizeable dowry is a powerful incentive for a man whose coffers are said to be virtually empty. Sir Lawrence is prepared to marry beneath him if he can get his hands on the type of sum Colonel Chadwick is rumored to have bequeathed Lucinda," Katherine said matter-of-factly.

"What does this have to do with Arabella?"

"As soon as Arabella's engagement was announced, Sir Lawrence made his own proposal and was happily accepted. Two weeks after his betrothal to Lucinda became official, Arabella's fiancé suddenly called the engagement off, citing a change of heart. Caroline Chadwick had a mind to sue the man for breach of promise, but Arabella begged her not to humiliate her any further, and in the end, her mother agreed."

"And you think Sir Lawrence planned the whole charade in order to secure Lucinda's hand in marriage without having to wait for Arabella to marry?"

"It would be a cruel trick to play on poor Arabella. She's such a sensitive soul, but the man she'd been engaged to is a known associate of Sir Lawrence Foxley."

Jason let out a low whistle and instantly checked himself. They were in a church, after all. "Would Lucinda condone such behavior in a man she's planning to marry?"

"I don't know. Lucinda teases Arabella mercilessly, and at times her jabs can be cruel, but she does love her sister. I'm sure of it."

"But does she love her enough to sacrifice a prestigious marriage?" Jason asked.

"I really couldn't say, but Sir Lawrence is quite the catch, and Lucinda is looking forward to becoming Lady Foxley."

"How's Arabella taking all this?"

"She seems—I don't know—withdrawn, I suppose. She's happy for Lucinda, of course, but given her own situation, having a wedding planned in her presence must be terribly painful."

"She is still very young. Surely there will be other proposals," Jason said. Arabella was a pretty girl, if a bit on the plump side, and he was sure her grandfather had left her a sizeable dowry as well.

"Caroline will drag her back to London for another Season, where she will be paraded before every eligible bachelor in the hope that her fortune will attract someone suitable. For someone as reticent as Arabella, that's the equivalent of being raked over hot coals, especially when her sister is not there to suffer alongside her, not that Lucinda was suffering. I think she enjoyed every moment of it and would gladly have come back for another Season if Sir Lawrence had failed to commit."

"You don't think Lucinda was pressured to accept Sir Lawrence, do you?" Jason asked.

"It has been Caroline Chadwick's greatest ambition to marry her daughters into noble families, and since you weren't interested in either of her girls, Caroline had to search for a title farther afield, but I doubt Caroline would force either of them to marry against their wishes. She does love her children," Katherine said.

"Was Harry not promised to Imogen Talbot since before he was out of short pants?" Jason asked.

"He was, but Harry didn't mind. Imogen is…was pretty, sweet, and obedient, the three qualities Harry wished for in a wife."

"Were they happy, do you think?" Jason inquired. He'd seen Harry and Imogen at church, but they didn't strike him as a young couple in love. Harry was solicitous, Imogen was demure, but for the amount of attention they paid each other, they might have been married for fifty years, and not affectionately so.

"I think Imogen was coming to accept her new position," Katherine replied cryptically.

"How do you mean, Katie?"

"Imogen was young and inexperienced when she married. I doubt she knew what to expect…" Katherine blushed and averted her eyes. "Well, you know."

"Yes," Jason said, amused by her embarrassment. "I know. But she knew Harry well before they married."

"Yes, but not in that way. I doubt he'd even kissed her before the wedding."

"I see. So, why is Sir Lawrence here?" Jason asked, wondering if it was customary for a bridegroom to visit his betrothed before the wedding and stay for longer than a few hours. As far as he knew, the wedding wasn't for a few weeks yet.

"The wedding is to be in London. That was one of Caroline's conditions. She wants to make sure it receives the proper attention and gets a write-up in *The Times*. I assume Caroline invited Sir Lawrence here to discuss the details, given that he doesn't have a mother to make the arrangements for him."

"Was Imogen not the mistress of the house, having married the master?" Jason asked, hard pressed to understand the family dynamic of the Chadwicks.

"She was."

"So, why is Caroline Chadwick ruling the roost?" Jason asked. He'd met Caroline several times and wondered if she had browbeaten poor Imogen into stepping aside. Could there have been a power struggle between the two women? Jason could hardly see Caroline strangling her daughter-in-law, but she could have made her life a misery.

"Imogen is…was happy to have someone take on all the responsibility. As long as Caroline was kind to her, she didn't mind letting her make all the difficult decisions."

"And was Caroline kind to her?"

"Yes, she was. She treated Imogen like one of her own daughters." Katherine tilted her head to the side and studied Jason for a moment. "You are not seriously suggesting that Imogen was killed by one of the family, are you?"

"I'm trying to learn as much as I can of Imogen's life," Jason replied, sidestepping the question.

"Jason, if Imogen was found in a Gypsy caravan, what possible difference does her everyday life and her relationship with her mother-in-law make to her death? Clearly she'd been accosted by a stranger." Katherine's eyes widened as realization dawned. "Oh God, Jason, was she violated?"

"No," Jason rushed to reassure her. "She was not sexually assaulted."

"Well, that's a relief, I suppose," Katherine said. "I would hate to think that she'd endured that before dying."

The church clock chimed, and Katherine jumped to her feet, as if a spring had been released inside. "I must be going. Father will want his luncheon as soon as he returns. He went to visit Mrs. Penrose. She's very poorly," Katherine threw over her shoulder as she headed for the door.

Jason hurried after her. "Katie, please be careful," he said as he caught up with her on the church porch. "We don't know who killed Imogen, or what has become of Moll. Please, promise me you won't go out alone."

Katherine stopped for a moment and gazed at him earnestly from behind her round spectacles. "I promise," she said solemnly. She put her hand on his arm. "I know you will find her killer. I have great faith in you."

"Thank you," Jason said, wishing he felt as confident in the outcome as she was.

Across the green, he could see about a dozen men gathered before the Red Stag. It seemed the search for Moll was about to commence.

Chapter 5

Daniel was under no illusion of the welcome he would receive at Chadwick Manor, and he wasn't wrong. Llewellyn, the Chadwicks' butler, who looked even more contemptuous than usual, advised Daniel that he should have called at the tradesmen's entrance rather than daring to come to the front door.

"I will do no such thing," Daniel replied, standing his ground. "I'm here on official police business, and you will inform Mr. Chadwick that I must see him immediately."

"Mr. Chadwick is not at home to visitors," Llewellyn intoned.

"I think you must be becoming hard of hearing, Mr. Llewellyn," Daniel said, staring down the old man. "I will see Mr. Chadwick now. If he's still abed, wake him."

Daniel shoved the door open, nearly unbalancing the shocked butler, and strode into the foyer, planting himself firmly in the middle. "Should I shout for Mr. Chadwick?" he asked, daring Llewellyn to test his resolve.

He could see the old man was tempted to let him try, but then years of conditioning kicked in, and he nodded in acquiescence. "If you would wait in the drawing room, I'll inform the master you're here," he said.

"Thank you," Daniel replied, and followed the man to the drawing room, where he wasn't invited to sit, but sat down nonetheless.

The house was surprisingly quiet despite the fact that one of the family was currently on her way to the basement mortuary at the Brentwood Police Station. How was it possible that no one was aware of Imogen's absence, not even her maid?

Losing his patience, Daniel stood and began to pace, the ticking of the carriage clock on the mantel like the tolling of church bells in his ears. He didn't relish this task, and the fact that the family was keeping him waiting was not going to make breaking the news to them any easier. At last, the door opened, and

Caroline Chadwick walked in. She wore a morning gown of pale yellow tastefully adorned with cream lace at the neckline and sleeves. Her auburn hair was pinned up, a few tendrils artfully framing her face. Caroline Chadwick was in her mid-forties, but she could have easily passed for a much younger woman, the vitality of her younger days having reasserted itself after the deaths of her husband and father-in-law, who'd made her life a lot more complicated than any woman's life should be. Daniel briefly wondered if the Birch Hill rumor mill had the right of it and Caroline was carrying on with her gamekeeper but dismissed the thought from his mind. It was none of his business, especially today, when the news he had to impart was about to shatter this family in a way no clandestine affair ever could.

Caroline stopped a few feet away from Daniel and pinned him with her less-than-welcoming gaze. "I assume something important has happened or you wouldn't be beating down my door at this ungodly hour, Inspector Haze."

"It's nearly noon, Mrs. Chadwick," Daniel pointed out, "and yes, something has happened. I would prefer to speak to your son, if I may."

"You may not," Caroline replied in her haughtiest tone. "Whatever you have to say can be said to me."

Since the death of Colonel Chadwick, Harry Chadwick was the master of Chadwick Manor, but Caroline clearly had no intention of surrendering control to her son or his wife. She was still very much in charge, the beautiful and spirited matriarch of the family.

"Very well," Daniel said, remembering to soften his tone. His irritation with the woman didn't make what he had to tell her any less tragic or painful. "Won't you have a seat?"

"I'll stand, thank you," she snapped. "The sooner you've said your piece, the sooner I can ask you to leave."

All right. Have it your way, Daniel thought, and plunged in. "Mrs. Chadwick, early this morning, the body of a young woman was discovered at the Gypsy campsite at Bloody Mead."

"What's that to do with me?"

"Quite a lot, actually," Daniel said gently. "The victim has been identified as your daughter-in-law, Mrs. Imogen Chadwick."

Caroline blanched, her hand going to her stomach. "Are you certain it's Imogen?" she rasped.

"I'm afraid I am," Daniel replied, taking a step toward the woman in case she swooned. "I have just come from the camp." He was about to tell her that he'd seen the remains but stopped himself, giving Caroline a moment to absorb the news.

Caroline staggered toward the settee and sank down, her shoulders sagging, her head bowed. She took several shaky breaths before lifting her face to glare at Daniel. "How did Imogen die?" she demanded.

Daniel was relieved that Caroline didn't waste time disputing the identity of the victim or demanding to see the body for herself. Daniel had known Imogen Talbot, as she had been known until a few months ago, all her life, so Caroline had correctly surmised he was telling her the truth. A formal identification would still need to take place, but it didn't have to be this morning.

"She was garroted."

"Dear God," Caroline whispered, her hand covering her mouth as if she were going to be sick. "I don't understand. How could this have happened?" She stared at Daniel, incomprehension clouding her gaze. "You said she was found at the Gypsy camp. What was she doing there? Why would they hurt her?" she cried shrilly.

"We don't know that they did."

"If that's where she was discovered, surely they're responsible," Caroline countered angrily. She needed to make sense of what had happened, and this was the most obvious conclusion, but Daniel wasn't convinced of the Romani's guilt. The most obvious answer wasn't always the correct one, and he had yet to uncover a motive for Imogen's death.

"The Romani have been camping in Bloody Mead for decades. They have never murdered anyone in cold blood," Daniel began.

"That we know of!" Caroline screeched.

"That we know of," Daniel agreed. "But I have interviewed everyone at the site, and as far as I can tell, they had no reason to hurt your daughter-in-law."

"And you think they'd tell you the truth, you foolish man? They're thieves and liars, the lot of them. You must arrest them before they flee. And they will flee; mark my words. They won't wait to be hanged for Imogen's death. Oh, my poor, poor girl," Caroline moaned.

"Mrs. Chadwick, I need to ask you a few questions," Daniel said as tactfully as he could.

Caroline glared at him defiantly but then marginally inclined her head, agreeing to his request.

"When was the last time you saw your daughter-in-law?" Daniel asked as he resumed his seat.

"Yesterday afternoon. She pleaded a headache and retired to her room. She wished to rest and asked not to be disturbed."

"Did no one bring her dinner?" Daniel asked.

Caroline shook her head. "Imogen hasn't been well," she said. She looked furtive for a moment, but then her shoulders sank in defeat. There was no point in hiding the truth now. "She was *enceinte*."

"How far along?" Daniel asked.

"Less than two months. Dr. Parsons confirmed it only last week."

"I see. So, Imogen claimed she was unwell and went up, and no one has checked on her, not even your son?"

"My son and his wife have separate bedrooms, as befits people of our class," Caroline replied haughtily, holding forth as if she were a member of the nobility, which she most certainly was not. The Chadwicks were *nouveau riche*, their money made in trade and coal over the past several decades.

Daniel nodded, resolving not to upset the woman any further. "Did no one realize she wasn't in her bedroom this morning?"

"Imogen usually summoned her maid when she woke. There was no reason to barge in and disturb her rest," Caroline replied miserably. "We had no reason to suspect she wasn't in her bed, asleep."

"Would no one have seen her leave the house?" Daniel asked. Surely, given the number of servants the Chadwicks employed, someone would have seen Imogen sneaking out.

"No one mentioned anything," Caroline said.

"And what did the rest of you do last evening?" Daniel asked.

"Are you suggesting we killed her?" Caroline cried, bright spots of color blooming in her cheeks.

"I'm suggesting no such thing, but I would like to have a clear picture of where everyone was from three o'clock on."

"Harry and Sir Lawrence—that's Lucinda's intended—were in the billiards room, having a game, I believe. I was in my sitting room, catching up on some correspondence. Then I had a rest until it was time to change for dinner."

"And your daughters?" Daniel asked.

"Arabella was sulking somewhere, and Lucinda planned to look over some bridal fashion plates. She wished to have some alterations made to her gown." Caroline paled, as though the realization that the wedding would have to be postponed had just dawned on her with devastating clarity.

Caroline raised her eyes to Daniel's face, grief finally defeating outrage, shock, and disbelief. She suddenly looked older, shrunken, as if the news had aged her in a matter of moments. Gone was the vibrant society matron, replaced by a grieving mother and grandmother-to-be.

"Did she suffer?" Caroline whispered. "Did she know what was happening?"

Some part of Daniel desperately wanted to lie to her, but she'd see the body within the next few days, and she'd know the truth.

"Yes, she did know, and she did suffer," Daniel replied gently, "but not for long. Death would have come quickly."

Caroline nodded. "If you've no objection, I will break the news to my son. He'll be devastated."

"As you wish," Daniel acquiesced. "Mrs. Chadwick, I will have to return to question the family and the staff."

"Is that really necessary?" Caroline demanded, the haughty matron once again. "Sir Lawrence—"

"Yes, I realize you have a guest, but there is no way for me to discover who killed your daughter-in-law without speaking with everyone she might have come in contact with on the last day of her life. I must reconstruct a timeline of events and recreate her movements."

She nodded. "I understand. You will catch whoever did this, won't you?" she asked, her eyes pleading with him to say yes. He'd never seen Caroline Chadwick brought so low, and despite her previous treatment of him, he felt a deep pity. Imogen had not been her own daughter, but he was sure she'd cared deeply for the girl, especially now that she had been about to make Caroline a grandmother and produce an heir to the Chadwick estate. Daniel would have liked to gauge Harry's reaction to the news, but he didn't insist on seeing the young man. The family deserved a few hours to grieve in private before the reality of the situation was driven home by his intrusive questions.

"Where is Imogen now?" Caroline asked. Daniel couldn't help noticing that she'd avoided using the term *body* or *remains*, so he replied in the same vein, respecting her inability to refer to Imogen as a corpse.

"She has been taken to the Brentwood Police Station."

"I trust she's being treated in a respectful manner," Caroline said, squaring her shoulders for battle. "There will be no postmortem. I forbid it."

Only Harry Chadwick, as the husband of the deceased, had the authority to forbid an autopsy, but Daniel saw no reason to argue with Caroline. Jason had already performed his examination, and even though it was too soon to tell that Imogen had been with child, he'd learned everything he needed to from the body. Even if Imogen had suffered from some underlying condition, it hadn't been the cause of death.

"Your wishes in this matter will be respected," Daniel said. "You may collect Imogen's body whenever you wish."

"Thank you, Inspector," Caroline said. "I appreciate your sensitivity."

"When may I return to question the family and staff?" Daniel asked, pressing his advantage while Caroline was feeling benevolent toward him.

"Tomorrow morning. Eleven o'clock. I will make sure you receive full cooperation."

"I appreciate that. You have my sincerest condolences."

Caroline nodded and wrapped her arms around her middle, as if to keep from falling apart. Daniel left her to her grief and walked into the foyer, closing the drawing room door softly behind him to give her a few moments of privacy. Llewellyn looked confused as he led Daniel toward the front door. He'd been in the Chadwicks' employ long enough to realize that something was terribly wrong, given the length of the interview and the sorrowful expression on Daniel's face.

"Good day, sir," Llewellyn said, for once forgetting to be rude.

Retrieving the dogcart from the stable yard, Daniel drove away. As a policeman, he was supposed to remain detached and focus on the details of the case, but he felt a deep sense of sorrow for the shy young woman whose life had only just begun and had ended in such a brutal, unexpected way. And he was also deeply concerned for Moll Brody. Where in blazes was she?

Chapter 6

"Were you able to learn anything useful?" Daniel asked as he joined Jason in the dining room of Redmond Hall. Having missed breakfast on account of the early morning summons, he was starving, and eternally grateful to Jason for anticipating this and holding off luncheon until he got there. Thankfully, Mr. Sullivan and his charge had opted for a schoolroom lunch, so Daniel and Jason could speak freely without fear of being interrupted.

Jason was just about to reply when Fanny arrived with the soup tureen and a plate of freshly baked bread. While Fanny served the soup, Daniel helped himself to a piece of bread, buttered it, and wolfed it down in two bites. Jason hardly noticed, but Fanny looked at him in amazement at his lack of table manners.

"Thank you, Fanny. That will be all for now," Jason said when Fanny chose to linger, refilling water glasses and moving the bread and butter further away from Daniel and closer to her master. Jason waited until she was out of earshot to share what he'd learned.

"According to Matty Locke, Sir Lawrence Foxley arrived in the village on Sunday afternoon with his coachman and valet."

"Yes, Caroline Chadwick mentioned his presence in the house," Daniel said as he turned his attention to the delicious consommé.

"Were the Chadwicks aware of Imogen's disappearance?" Jason asked as he reached for a piece of bread.

Daniel laid down his spoon, realizing that the hollow feeling in his stomach had little to do with hunger. "They had no idea, Jason. According to Caroline Chadwick, Imogen, who was in the early stages of pregnancy, had not been feeling well and retired early, asking not to be disturbed. They simply assumed she was resting and would summon her maid when she was ready to either rise from her bed or eat something."

"Harry Chadwick never checked on his pregnant wife?" Jason asked, his surprise evident.

"It would seem not."

"And her maid?"

"I will be interviewing the family and staff tomorrow morning. I'll know more then."

"Do you think they'll be forthcoming?" Jason asked.

"I hope so, for Imogen's sake, but I expect the family will leave out anything that's not a verifiable fact, and the servants will take their lead from their masters. If Caroline Chadwick encourages them to be frank, they'll tell me what they know. If she doesn't, then they might withhold pertinent information."

"Then let me fill in the gaps, so to speak," Jason offered. He waited until Fanny, who had returned, cleared the soup plates and placed a platter of cold salmon garnished with dill mayonnaise and accompanied by roasted potatoes on the table before departing.

"I stopped by the vicarage after speaking to Matty," Jason began. "Katherine was able to provide some context for Sir Lawrence's sudden visit and also explain something of the family dynamic."

"Thank you. That's bound to be helpful, knowing how close she is to both the Talbots and the Chadwicks."

"That's what I thought," Jason said. "As you know, Imogen Talbot and Harry Chadwick were married a few months ago, an arrangement that had been agreed on years ago by the families. It wasn't a love match, but they got on, probably more due to Imogen's sweet disposition than Harry's desire to make the marriage work. With Harry accounted for, Caroline Chadwick turned her attention to her daughters, taking them to London for the Season on a husband-hunting expedition. Arabella was the first to get engaged, with Lucinda a close second, but Arabella's fiancé turned tail shortly after Lucinda and Sir Lawrence's betrothal was formally announced, leaving the poor girl shocked and humiliated. Arabella's young man is a known associate of Sir Lawrence," Jason said, his gaze meeting Daniel's across the table.

"I don't see how that ties in with Imogen's murder, but any insight into the days and months leading up to the murder can be significant."

"Not if Imogen was killed by the Romani," Jason speculated. "Daniel, there's something I need to tell you. In confidence. Moll's natural father was Romani. He was a Lee."

Daniel set down his fork, his mouth slack with shock. "What? Who told you that?"

"Davy Brody."

"Good Lord," Daniel exclaimed. "Well, that casts a whole new light on the investigation, doesn't it?" He felt as if a yawning chasm had just opened in his chest. He hadn't really thought Moll's disappearance was connected to the murder, but now that she was directly linked to the Gypsy tribe, her absence was impossible to ignore. "We need to find Moll. Or her remains."

"But why would the Romani kill Moll? And why now?" Jason asked, lowering his voice when Fanny entered the room to clear away the remnants of their luncheon.

"Perhaps she posed a threat," Daniel suggested as soon as the door closed behind the maid.

"What sort of threat? Moll is twenty-one years old," Jason said. "This is all ancient history."

"Not to her," Daniel countered.

"All right, let's suppose you're correct and Moll has been made aware of her parentage. How would that lead to her murder?"

"I honestly don't know," Daniel replied, shaking his head. "Nor do I know what Moll's paternity might have to do with Imogen Chadwick, but we need to speak to the Romani again. They have lied to us, one and all."

"Daniel, did we interview anyone named Andrei?" Jason asked, his brow furrowed as he tried to attach the name to the person.

"No. Is that the name of Moll's father?"

Jason nodded. "Supposing the man had died recently, perhaps he'd left something of value behind, and if he had other children, they may not have wanted to share their portion with Moll."

"That's an interesting suggestion. Do you think he would have acknowledged Moll in his will? Do Gypsies even have wills, or anything to leave in them?" Daniel asked as he took out his handkerchief. He removed his spectacles and cleaned them thoroughly, something he did when he needed a moment to think.

"I don't know anything about the Romani lifestyle," Jason replied. "I'd never even heard of them until this morning."

"Are there no Gypsies in America?"

"I've never come across any. Most people in America want land. It's the ultimate prize. Few would keep traveling from place to place when they can settle down and build a life."

"This *is* their life," Daniel replied, having replaced his glasses on his nose. "I could never be happy traipsing from place to place with no bricks and mortar to call home, but they swear by it. What we see as rootlessness, they see as freedom."

"I suppose freedom comes in different forms. Sometimes being bound to a place is more of a prison sentence than a promise of security."

"Is that why you came to England?" Daniel asked softly, wondering if Jason's home had become a place he wished to leave behind.

"I didn't think so at the time. I made the journey to see to my grandfather's estate, but I suppose I could have accomplished everything remotely, had I been willing to devote a year or more to allowing the lawyers on either side of the Atlantic to take the necessary steps. I did think Micah and I could benefit from a change of scene and put some distance between ourselves and the experiences that had brought us together. But now that you mention it, I suppose the house in New York had become something of a prison, and the prospect of seeing new places and having fresh experiences was a sort of freedom."

Daniel nodded in understanding. "And do you feel free?"

"I'll never be free of the memories, but I am happy," Jason admitted shyly.

"So am I," Daniel replied. "And worried."

"All will be well," Jason assured him. "Sarah is healthy and strong, and you will get to meet your baby very soon. In the meantime, do you want to return to the encampment?" Jason asked.

"Not today, but I would appreciate it if you'd come with me tomorrow. I'll collect you around nine?"

"Of course," Jason said. "Where are you off to now?"

"I must report to Detective Inspector Coleridge and apprise him of the situation. And you?"

"I will recruit Shawn Sullivan, Roger Henley, and Joe Marin to help with the search for Moll. I do hope we find her," Jason said.

"So do I, Jason. So do I."

Chapter 7

By the time Daniel arrived at the station, it was nearly three o'clock. Sergeant Flint was manning the desk, a newspaper spread before him, his pipe filling the vestibule with fragrant tobacco smoke.

"Good afternoon, Inspector Haze," Flint drawled, his gaze still on the paper.

"I would like to speak to Detective Inspector Coleridge," Daniel said. "Is he available?"

"Nah. Been closeted with the commissioner for the past hour. I reckon they should be done soon. There's tea in the pot," Sergeant Flint added, tilting his head toward a brown earthenware pot on his desk.

"Thank you, no. I'll just wait," Daniel said, and settled in a chair meant for visitors.

"I saw the lovely that's been brought in from Birch Hill. Garroted. Shame, that."

"I knew her. She was a decent woman," Daniel said, but the observation felt false on his tongue. A woman was someone who'd lived, who'd had experiences, but Imogen Chadwick had been hardly more than a girl at the time of her death. Until her marriage, her world had been limited to the schoolroom and the occasional outing with her parents. It saddened him to think of the many years stolen from her.

"Have you made an arrest?" Flint asked, interrupting Daniel's reverie.

"Not yet," Daniel said. "I don't even have a suspect at present."

Sergeant Flint bared his teeth in an ugly snarl. "Arrest them all. Burn down their bloody caravans and drive them off for good. They're like vermin; they keep breeding unless you exterminate them."

"Are you proposing we execute an entire group of people?" Daniel asked, aghast by the sergeant's comments.

"If that's what's needed. They're savages, they are. Not like decent English folk."

"I think that's a bit harsh, don't you?" Daniel protested.

"Not at all. They are not like us and never will be."

"They are people, aren't they?" Daniel demanded, outraged.

"Having two arms, two legs, and a cock don't make someone a man. You know how I know that?" Sergeant Flint demanded. "Answer me this. When a man needs a new horse, what does he do?"

"Buys one."

"Exactly. He buys a horse. He doesn't steal one. And when a man has a mind to marry, what does he do? He finds himself a woman of good character."

"And what does a Gypsy do?" Daniel asked, curious what codswallop Sergeant Flint was about to spew.

"He doesn't marry. He fucks his sister instead. They're all inbred, I tell you. Each and every one of them. That's why they have no morals and no understanding of right and wrong."

Daniel was about to reply but was saved from getting embroiled in an argument by the arrival of the commissioner, who jammed his hat onto his head and exited the station after nodding briefly to the two men. Detective Inspector Coleridge stepped out into the corridor and beckoned for Daniel to join him in his office.

DI Coleridge took a seat behind his desk. He looked tired and thoroughly irritated. "Please tell me you have some good news, Haze."

"I don't, sir."

DI Coleridge sighed heavily. "Well, I don't suppose this day can get any worse."

Daniel didn't ask what the inspector was referring to. Given that the commissioner had just left and hadn't looked to be in a jovial mood was explanation enough.

"I take it you knew the victim?" Coleridge asked kindly.

"I did. The family will not allow a postmortem. They'll send an undertaker to collect the body."

DI Coleridge nodded. "That's fine. Not like there's any great mystery to how she died."

"No, the cause of death is obvious, but we haven't found the murder weapon," Daniel admitted.

"And what do you suppose was used?"

"Lord Redmond believes she was garroted with a wire, sir."

"What are your thoughts, Inspector?" DI Coleridge asked. "Did the Romani kill her? Everyone here thinks it's an open and shut case."

"I don't know if I agree with that, sir."

"Why not? She was found in a caravan. Who else would have killed her?"

"I can't answer that until I establish the motive. I can't see how Imogen Chadwick posed a threat to anyone, but some new information has just come to light, and I will need to interview the Travelers again."

"What sort of information?"

"A young woman is missing. Moll Brody is the niece of the publican at the Red Stag. He's confided to Lord Redmond that Moll's natural father was a Gypsy."

DI Coleridge leaned back in his seat and considered this bit of news. "Well, now. That rather changes things, doesn't it?"

"I'm sure it does, but I don't yet see how," Daniel admitted.

"Might the victim have been mistaken for this Moll Brody?" DI Coleridge asked.

"No. Moll is dark-haired, buxom, and boisterous. The exact opposite of Imogen Chadwick."

"Did the two women share a bond of some sort?"

"Not that I know of, sir. In fact, I don't think they so much as said a word to each other in years, if ever."

DI Coleridge shook his head in dismay. "Clearly, one or both of these women posed a threat to the Romani. Collar the murderer, Haze, and quickly. People don't need much to fuel their prejudices, especially in a situation where there's little doubt of guilt. I don't want to have to arrest Englishmen for murder or assault on the Gypsies. That will turn the masses against the police, and we need them working with us, not against us."

"You think the Romani are now a target?" Daniel asked. Despite Sergeant Flint's derogatory comments, he hadn't considered the possibility until that moment.

"Don't you?"

"Can we not offer them some sort of protection?" Daniel asked, realizing how ridiculous he sounded.

"We barely have enough coppers to maintain order in Brentwood. You think we can afford to guard Gypsies day and night? They'll just have to see to themselves, won't they? I just hope they don't move on before we make an arrest."

"I've asked them not to leave the area."

Detective Inspector Coleridge let out a guffaw. "You really are naïve, aren't you, Haze? What's there to stop them?"

"Not much," Daniel muttered as he stood to leave.

"Keep me informed and let me know if you need backup when you question them. And for God's sake, find the missing woman. She just might be the key to this murder."

"Will do, sir."

Daniel hurried toward the exit, eager to get home.

"Any messages?" he asked Tilda when he arrived home. "Have they found Moll?"

Tilda wouldn't have left the house all afternoon, but like most servants, she had her ear to the ground and would know of any developments long before Daniel got word, most likely from the fruit and veg man, or the butcher, or any other tradesman who happened to call by.

"No, sir. They're still searching."

"Where's Mrs. Haze?"

"She's in the garden, sir."

Daniel handed over his coat and hat and headed for the garden, looking forward to spending a few peaceful minutes in Sarah's colorful oasis. She was sitting on her favorite bench beneath the beech tree, her face dappled by sunlight, a book in her hand.

Sarah set aside the book and looked up when he approached, her smile of welcome fading when she saw the look on his face.

"That bad?" she asked, her hand instinctively going to her belly, as if she could protect their unborn child from any unnecessary unpleasantness.

"I want to forget this day ever happened," Daniel replied, reaching for her other hand. Normally, he would share his fears and concerns with Sarah, but it was his duty to protect her from harm and shield her from anything that might upset her, especially now that she was days away from the birth of their baby. He hoped Sarah hadn't already heard the details of Imogen's death. The image of that poor young woman would haunt her, more so if she discovered Imogen had been pregnant at the time of her death.

"We shan't speak of it, then," Sarah said, her eyes filled with sympathy. They settled into a comfortable silence, the late afternoon sun gilding the garden in a golden haze and the sound of birdsong making up for the lack of conversation.

"What do you think of Charles?" Sarah suddenly asked.

"Sorry. Charles who?"

Sarah laughed softly. "I meant as a potential name for the baby."

"I thought you didn't want to decide until you saw the baby," Daniel said carefully, not wishing to upset her.

"I don't, but I'd like to have a few options prepared."

"I like Charles," Daniel replied. "It's a fine name."

"What about Caius? It means *rejoice*."

"I think I prefer Charles. Caius is a bit…" Daniel let the sentence trail of.

"What?"

"Pompous."

Sarah laughed again. "I expected you to say that."

"Are you set on a name that starts with C?"

Sarah shrugged. "I'm trying out a few names to see how I feel about them."

Daniel sighed. "Sarah, I'll be happy with whatever name you like."

It had been Daniel's desire to name their son Felix. He'd liked the name, and Sarah had agreed, even though she'd been partial to naming him Leo. Daniel had joked that both names were in the feline family. If only their little boy had had nine lives, but he was long gone, killed in an accident nearly four years before, and nothing would bring him back. Daniel didn't care what the child was called as long as it made old bones.

"You mean it?" Sarah asked playfully.

"I mean it. If you want to name the baby Caius, then Caius he shall be."

"I'll think on it," Sarah said, her expression dreamy. Daniel was in no doubt that she was envisioning calling out to a little boy, testing out the name as if their son had already been born. Did she see Felix in her mind's eye when she pictured this new baby?

"Have you chosen a name for a girl?" Daniel asked.

"I have, but I won't tell you just yet. Since you said it's up to me, then there's no need to win your approval," Sarah joked.

"No need at all," Daniel agreed, and drew her to him, kissing the top of her head. *Dear Lord, please protect them both*, Daniel prayed as he held Sarah close. He didn't think he'd survive another loss.

Chapter 8

The sun was setting by the time the search party returned to the Red Stag, crimson and gold streaks painting the sky, though its glory was lost on the disheartened men, who were tired and subdued, their gazes downcast as they shuffled into the tavern.

"Drinks are on me, lads," Davy Brody said. Normally, a statement like that would be met with noisy approval, but today no one commented on Davy's generosity. After hours of combing the countryside, the men were parched, and a pint was their due.

"What can I get ye, yer lordship?" Davy asked as Jason approached the bar.

"Nothing, thank you," Jason replied. "We will find her," he said with more conviction than he felt. They hadn't found Moll, but then they hadn't discovered her remains either. Jason thought there was hope in that.

Davy shrugged, unconvinced. "Sure you won't have a drink?" he asked instead, reverting to the role he was comfortable in.

"No. Goodnight, Mr. Brody."

"Thank you for your assistance, yer lordship."

Jason left the men to enjoy well-earned pints and a brief rest and set off for home. He was surprised to see Katherine hurrying toward him, her hand on her bonnet to keep it from coming off in her haste. The sun had just dipped behind the vicarage, so Jason couldn't make out Katherine's features, but his heart leaped with concern, and he rushed toward her.

"Katie, are you all right?" Jason demanded. "What's happened?"

Katherine took a moment to catch her breath, then smiled up at him. "I'm absolutely fine. I was watching from the parlor window, waiting for the search party to return. And then I saw you coming out of the Stag. There's something I forgot to mention when we spoke this afternoon, and I think it might be important."

"Tell me," Jason said as they turned toward the vicarage and began to walk slowly across the village green.

"Jason, I don't want to point the finger at anyone, certainly not without evidence to support any wrongdoing, but Moll has been stepping out with someone."

"She has? Who?"

"Tristan Carmichael."

"And who is he?" Jason couldn't recall hearing the name before.

"I'm not sure if you're aware, but Davy Brody had been involved in smuggling before you came to the village," Katherine said.

"Yes, Inspector Haze mentioned it. Said Brody paid a hefty fine and was lucky to escape a prison sentence, from what I recall."

Katherine nodded. "There's a reason Davy never went to prison. The case was closed before it had a chance to go to trial."

"Why was that?"

"Because Lance Carmichael wanted it so."

"And how is it that this Lance Carmichael has such power?" Jason asked.

Katherine shook her head. "I really don't know. I only know he's not a man to be crossed. I heard the squire say so to my father at the time. And Tristan is Lance Carmichael's son."

"Are you suggesting that Davy is still in the smuggling business?"

"I honestly don't know. I can only tell you what I saw."

"And what was that?"

"I came across Moll and Tristan walking in the lane when I was coming back from visiting the Caulfields last week. They looked very eh…close. And then I saw them again shortly before Imogen was murdered."

"How did you know the man was Tristan Carmichael?" Jason asked.

"Moll introduced me to him."

"Hmm," Jason said, considering this new angle. "I'll have to share what you've told me with Inspector Haze."

"Of course," Katherine said. "But don't be surprised if he's not pleased to hear it."

"I won't be," Jason muttered, sensing the truth of Katherine's warning.

They had reached the vicarage and Jason was just about to say goodnight when Reverend Talbot yanked the door open.

"Katherine, come inside this minute," he hissed, looking around to see if anyone had seen Katherine and Jason together. There was no one about.

"I'm coming, Father. I just had to tell Jason something important," Katherine explained patiently.

"Nothing is so important it couldn't wait until tomorrow." He glared at Jason. "Goodnight, your lordship," he said tartly.

"Reverend," Jason said, tipping his hat. "Goodnight, Katie," he whispered as soon as Reverend Talbot turned his back.

Katherine blew him a kiss and disappeared inside, no doubt to hear a lengthy lecture on the propriety of speaking to a man alone in the evening in full view of the village.

Jason walked the short distance to Redmond Hall and settled in the drawing room with a brandy, his mind teeming with questions. Why would someone want to kill Imogen Chadwick? What danger could she possibly have posed to anyone, especially to the Romani, who'd be gone from Birch Hill in a few weeks, not to return again until next year? Who benefited from her death? And how was Moll involved? Was her connection to the Romani a factor, and was her disappearance related to Imogen Chadwick's murder?

The door opened, and Micah came in. He took the armchair opposite Jason and looked at him, his blue gaze earnest and worried. "Are you sad, Captain?" Micah asked. He always called Jason by the rank he'd held when they'd met.

"Yes," Jason replied.

"It's not good to be by yourself when you're sad. You told me that many times when I wanted to stay alone in my room."

"I'm not very good company right now," Jason replied.

"That's all right. Go ahead, tell me," Micah invited. At twelve, he was mature beyond his years. The years he'd served as a drummer boy for his father and brother's regiment and the time he'd spent at Andersonville Prison had robbed him of his childhood, and he was more of a man than some adults Jason knew.

"I just keep thinking about it, Micah, trying to understand. Who would want to hurt Imogen Chadwick? She was so…"

"Colorless," Micah supplied.

Jason looked at him with surprise. Now that Micah had said it, the adjective fit perfectly. Imogen had been colorless, nearly invisible in her desire to blend into the woodwork. Jason couldn't recall the last time he'd actually heard her speak.

"Which makes it all the more incomprehensible," Jason replied.

"Does it?" Micah asked, looking at Jason as if he were the adult and Jason the child. "You've seen men slaughter each other on the battlefield, and you've seen men loot and burn and assault defenseless women off the battlefield. You know what people are capable of, and they don't need much provocation, do they?" Micah asked sadly. Some part of him still couldn't believe that the people he'd grown up with, had sat next to in church, had turned on Mary when she'd helped a wounded Confederate soldier, and burned their farm to the ground, leaving the Donovans with nothing to call their own.

"You're right, of course. People don't need much to shrug off the cloak of civility and revert to the animals they are underneath."

Micah nodded. "Want a game of chess?" he asked.

"Isn't it your bedtime?" Jason countered.

"I was hoping you wouldn't notice."

"Well, I did. Off with you. Goodnight."

"Goodnight," Micah grumbled.

Jason threw back the remainder of his brandy and got to his feet. It was too early for him to retire, but he was more than ready to leave this day behind. Hours of walking through the woods and fields had tired him, and an early night suddenly seemed like a fine idea. But just as he approached the door of his bedroom, Jason was waylaid by Mary. She looked upset, and her hands were clasped before her in a universal gesture of distress.

"Mary, are you all right? Is it Liam?"

She nodded miserably. "I think he's ill. He's feverish, and he's barely eaten anything all day. I'm frightened," she whispered.

"Let's have a look," Jason said in his most soothing tone. He followed Mary into her bedroom down the corridor. Mary had been offered the use of the nursery and the services of a nursemaid, but she had insisted on keeping Liam with her, a decision Jason could understand. She needed to be close to him, and the child benefited from his mother's constant attention. At just over a year old, he was healthy, strong, and surprisingly cunning.

Liam lay in the cradle that had once belonged to Jason's father, his dark eyes clouded with misery. His face was flushed, his chin sticky with drool. Jason laid a hand on Liam's forehead, then moved it down to his neck to take his pulse. It was steady. His chest rose and fell rhythmically, so no respiratory distress, Jason concluded. He watched the child for a moment. Liam's legs were still, which was a good sign. Babies tended to kick their legs when they had a stomachache. Jason poured some water into a basin and washed his hands before inserting his finger into the baby's mouth.

"What are you doing?" Mary cried.

Jason felt around for moment, then pulled his hand away, amused by Liam's grimace of outrage. "His molars are coming in."

"His what?" Mary asked.

"His back teeth. This is often accompanied by fever, drooling, and general crankiness. I imagine it's not pleasant for him. He just needs a bit of comforting," Jason said as he picked up the baby and held him against his chest. "There now," he crooned. "That's better, isn't it? Let's take a walk, shall we?" He walked back and forth until Liam rested his head against Jason's shoulder and began to nod off.

"Thank you, Captain. I'm so relieved it's nothing serious. Should I order a bottle of Mrs. Winslow's Soothing Syrup?" Mary asked. "I have seen it advertised in the newspaper."

"Absolutely not," Jason replied. "It's nothing but morphine. Liam will feel better in a few days, once the teeth have cut through. I'll ask Mrs. Dodson to mash some cloves. Clove oil has soothing properties. Liam probably won't like the taste, but it will give him some relief and help him sleep through the night."

"Thank you," Mary said again. She sat down on the bed, her shoulders slumping in dejection.

"What it is?" Jason asked softly. The child was half asleep, drooling freely on Jason's sleeve, but he ignored the sticky wetness and focused on Mary instead.

"I wish Clayton was here, is all," Mary said miserably. "I think about him all the time. I miss him," she whispered, her eyes misting with tears. "He never even knew I was with child. He died not knowing he was to be a father."

"Mary, I know you're still grieving, but someday, the pain will begin to dull. You'll meet someone new and build a life together. Maybe even have more children."

"Can I ask you something?" Mary asked, looking up at Jason shyly.

"Of course."

"Does Mr. Sullivan have family in London?"

"I think his family is in Dublin," Jason replied. "Why do you ask?"

"If he has no family in London, whom does he go to see on his days off?" Mary asked, watching Jason in a way that made him distinctly uncomfortable.

"A friend, I presume," Jason replied noncommittally.

"A lady friend?" Mary asked.

Jason lowered his gaze, as if to check if Liam was asleep, but in reality, he needed a moment to formulate an appropriate response. He couldn't tell Mary the truth. Homosexuality was no longer a hanging offense, but it was still a crime punishable by a prison sentence. He had no right to put Shawn in danger, no matter how much he trusted that Mary would tell no one.

"I thought you were interested in Roger," Jason finally said, sidestepping the question. He didn't really believe Mary had any designs on Roger Henley, but Jason had seen some warm looks directed Mary's way and assumed Roger had either lost interest or been rejected by Moll, which would make sense if Moll and Tristan Carmichael were courting.

Mary scoffed. "He's sweet on me, but I would never step out with the likes of him. I've seen it often enough back home. A girl thinks her fella's drinking is just a bit of youthful high spirits, and then she finds herself married to a drunk who spends his wages on booze and uses his fists on his wife and children. No, thank you," Mary said hotly. "I'll not have me a drinking man. A teetotaler for me," she announced. "Or no one at all."

Jason smiled at her passion. She was young, but she'd seen enough of life to know what to look for in a man. "I'm very glad to hear that. You're right, Roger would not make a good husband."

Mary's gaze turned pleading. "Does Mr. Sullivan have a sweetheart, Captain? I really would rather know."

"Mary, Mr. Sullivan is a fine man, but he isn't for you," Jason said softly. She looked like she was about to ask why but was too proud to pursue the matter any further, which was a relief, since Jason had no good reason to give her.

"In any case, I've no wish to marry an Englishman," Mary suddenly said, having evidently given up on Shawn Sullivan. "If I do, I'll have to stay here, won't I?"

"Do you wish to return to the States?" Jason asked, surprised by the turn the conversation had taken.

Mary's head bobbed up and down. "I miss home. I don't belong here," she said, looking at him imploringly. "Everyone treats me like a pariah."

"I'm sure they don't," Jason replied patiently.

"I'm a Catholic Irishwoman from Maryland who lives with an American nobleman whose hobbies include solving murders and performing autopsies for the police," Mary reminded him. "I don't exactly fit in."

"Are you suggesting I'm an oddity?" Jason asked, arching his brows.

Mary giggled. "Aren't you? If not for your title and money, no one would so much as say good day to you."

Jason laughed softly. "I won't argue with you there. But seriously, if you wish to go home, just say the word. I will pay for your passage and make sure you and Liam want for nothing. Ever," Jason promised.

"If it wasn't for Micah, I'd have gone back already, but he's so happy here," Mary said. "He's a proper little gentleman."

"Hardly," Jason replied, chuckling to himself.

"You know what I mean. He has options here, a future. What will he do back in the States?"

"Have you spoken to Micah of your desire to return?" Jason asked. He carefully lowered Liam into the crib, glad the child hadn't woken.

"No, not yet. I don't want to upset him."

"Mary, this is Micah's home. He can remain here for as long as he wishes. I will see to his education. You needn't worry."

"But he wouldn't want to be parted from me," Mary said wistfully. "We're each other's only living family."

Jason sighed. "I can't tell you what to do. You and Micah must decide for yourselves. I will respect your wishes and help you in any way I can."

Mary nodded. "Thank you, Captain. I knew you'd understand."

"I do, but that doesn't mean I like it. I consider you and Micah my family. I would miss you," Jason said, and wished he hadn't. It wasn't fair to burden Mary with his feelings. She had enough to deal with.

"You are a very kind man," Mary said. Jason hadn't expected it, but she stood on her tiptoes and kissed his cheek. "And I love you," she said simply. "Goodnight, Captain."

"Goodnight," Jason said, embarrassed by Mary's show of emotion. "Sleep well," he mumbled, and fled.

Chapter 9

Thursday, May 9

Jason was ready to go by the time Daniel's dogcart appeared at the end of the gravel driveway. He stepped outside and waited for the cart to approach, noting the rigid set of Daniel's shoulders and the downward turn of his mouth. Daniel was not a man who grew easily dispirited during the course of an investigation, but this case was close to home, and he was emotionally involved.

"Good morning," Daniel said as he brought the cart to a stop.

"Is it?" Jason asked as he climbed in.

"Not particularly. DI Coleridge is concerned that the villagers will take matters into their own hands if we don't make an arrest soon."

Jason nodded, recalling Micah's prophetic words. "We'd best solve this quickly, then."

"Any word on Moll's whereabouts?"

"The search party was out for more than eight hours but found no trace of her."

"Do you think she's dead, Jason?" Daniel asked.

"If she is, then her remains are well hidden, unlike those of Imogen Chadwick. Not only was Imogen left where she was killed, but the crime was reported to the police."

Daniel turned to look at Jason, his eyes widening behind the lenses of his spectacles. "Are you suggesting there are two killers?"

"I think there could be several different possibilities," Jason said. "First: the killer acted on the spur of the moment and took his or her opportunity when they saw it, killing Imogen in the caravan and then possibly killing Moll someplace else and in a different way."

"I wish we had the means to dredge the river," Daniel said. "If the killer weighed down Moll's body with rocks and threw her in, we'll never find her," he said. "What's the second possibility?"

"The second is that Moll's disappearance has nothing to do with Imogen Chadwick's death, and we are looking at two unrelated events."

"That happened on the same day in a village the size of Birch Hill?" Daniel asked, incredulous. "What are the odds?"

"It seems Moll has a young man. Katherine saw them together, and Moll had even introduced them, so Katherine was able to provide me with a name."

"Did she, indeed?" Daniel asked, a hint of a smile appearing on his normally serious face. "Who is he?"

"Tristan Carmichael."

Daniel turned to stare at Jason, his face slack with astonishment. "You're joking!"

"Sorry, no. Is it as bad as that? Katherine did say his father is well connected."

"You could say that. The man is a thug, a known criminal."

"So, why isn't he behind bars if his activities are known to the authorities?"

"Because he owns the authorities," Daniel replied. "No one will dare touch him."

"What hold does he have over them?" Jason asked.

"Fear," Daniel replied angrily. "Lance Carmichael started out life as Bobby Huggins, youngest son of a two-bit smuggler. He joined the family business when he was hardly older than Micah. The smugglers brought goods from France, Holland, and Belgium up the Blackwater River and hid them in taverns along the shore until the goods could be disposed of. Unlike his father and brothers, Bobby quickly moved up the ranks, and by the time he was twenty-one had styled himself Lance Carmichael and branched out into several lucrative sidelines. He owns brothels, opium dens, gambling halls, and Lord only knows what else. If Carmichael needs to silence someone or make sure the outcome of a trial is favorable, he uses blackmail. If that fails, terrible accidents befall family members of magistrates and inspectors who refuse to be cowed."

"I see," Jason said. "And the son?"

"Not as ruthless as the father, by all accounts, but a chip off the old block, so to speak. He's in up to his neck, which his father is trying valiantly to keep out of the noose."

"And this is the man Moll has chosen for a sweetheart," Jason said, shaking his head in disbelief. "Do you think Lance Carmichael would approve of a match between his son and Davy Brody's niece?"

"I highly doubt that. Lance has two daughters who've married into the gentry. They play at being respectable. I can't see Lance Carmichael giving Tristan his blessing, especially if he became aware of Moll's true parentage."

"Will you interview Lance Carmichael?" Jason asked.

"Not if I don't have to, but I will have to speak to both Davy Brody and Tristan Carmichael."

Daniel's face grew even more serious as the Romani encampment came into view. He stopped the cart, and the two men climbed out and walked toward the clearing, their progress observed with obvious fear and mistrust.

"You speak to Zamfira while I re-interview Bogdan," Daniel suggested.

Chapter 10

When Daniel took a seat on an upturned bucket next to Bogdan Lee, everyone melted away, returning to their caravans or focusing on outside chores, but Daniel was sure he was being watched and the conversation would be overheard. Bogdan patted the dog they'd seen at the camp the previous day but didn't say anything, waiting for Daniel to speak.

"I'll get straight to the point," Daniel said.

"Please do."

"Moll Brody is missing, and it has come to my attention that her father was Romani."

Bogdan nodded sadly. The search party would have come to the camp, so he had to be aware of Moll's disappearance. "Yes, Moll Brody was a *didikko*."

"What is that?" Daniel asked. The term did not sound flattering.

"It means she was half-Romani," Bogdan explained.

"Her father was Andrei Lee. Relation of yours?"

"My brother. He died a couple of years ago."

"And did everyone here know that Moll was Andrei's daughter?" Daniel asked.

"It was common knowledge, yes."

"Did Moll know?"

Bogdan shook his head. "I don't believe so."

"Had she had any contact with Andrei before he died?"

"Not really. He kept his distance, but he liked it when she came. He loved her," Bogdan added.

"And did Andrei have other children?" Daniel asked.

"Yes. Zamfira is his daughter."

"I thought Zamfira is your daughter-in-law."

"She is. She's married to my oldest son. Yes, they are first cousins," Bogdan said in response to Daniel's look of incomprehension. "Look, Inspector, everyone has always known about Moll. They felt no animosity toward her. Moll Brody had no power to hurt them."

"What about Andrei's wife? Did she feel as benevolent toward her husband's love child as her daughter did?"

"Andrei had a relationship with Rachel Brody before he married Alba. She wasn't threatened by it."

"Did your brother leave anything of value when he died?" Daniel asked.

"Whatever he left belongs to his wife and daughter. He did not leave anything to Moll, so no, Inspector, neither Alba nor Zamfira had any reason to resent her."

"You make it all sound so amicable," Daniel said, wondering if the old man was lying through his teeth.

"It was. No one here has any reason to harm Moll Brody. No one."

"And did Moll come by the encampment the day before yesterday?" Daniel asked, watching the man intently.

"No, she did not. We have not seen her since we arrived."

"What breed of dog is that?" Daniel asked, watching the docile animal.

Bogdan shrugged. "I don't know. A mutt. His name is Borzo."

"I noticed that Borzo didn't bark when Lord Redmond and I arrived just now."

Bogdan smiled at the dog indulgently. "He's useless as a guard dog. He's so accustomed to people coming and going, he doesn't raise the alarm."

"Are you suggesting he wouldn't have barked if there had been a stranger in the camp?"

"Only if he found the person threatening. Borzo is too friendly for his own good and trusts everyone, especially if they offer him a treat." The dog set out to prove Bogdan right, taking off toward a young boy who was holding out a piece of bacon and calling to the dog. Borzo scarfed down the bacon and licked the boy's fingers, making him laugh.

"Thank you," Daniel said, and rose to his feet. He hoped Jason had fared better.

Chapter 11

Jason studied the beautiful young woman seated across from him. She had invited him into her caravan but had left the door open, the view of the sky and the fresh breeze blowing through the door making Jason feel less confined in the narrow space. Now that he knew of Moll's heritage, he thought he spotted a resemblance between the two women, but that was probably just his mind playing tricks.

Zamfira tilted her head and smiled at Jason. "Are you just going to sit there and look at me all day?" she asked playfully.

"Did you know Moll Brody was half-Romani?" Jason asked.

"Yes. Moll is my half-sister," Zamfira said. "I've always known about her. Everyone has."

"And how do you feel about your sister?"

"I like her. In a different world, we might have been close."

"Why did no one ever tell her the truth?"

"My father thought it would be unkind to make her question everything she knew about herself and her life."

"The man she believes to be her father ran out on her mother before the wedding," Jason pointed out.

"Yes, I know, but that version is still better than the truth. Few people would relish the knowledge that they're a Gypsy bastard. Better to be an English bastard any day."

"Did Moll come to see you since you arrived?"

Zamfira shook her head. "No, but I saw her."

"When and where?"

"It was on Tuesday, around three. I had gone to look for evening primrose. It usually grows by the roadside. I use it to make oil," Zamfira explained.

Jason nodded. He'd used oil of evening primrose himself to treat Dodson's eczema.

"I saw Moll walking with a man."

"Did she see you?"

"Yes. She waved to me and called out a greeting."

"Can you describe the man?" Jason asked.

"He was fair and had light eyes. He was well dressed," Zamfira added.

"Did you detect any animosity between them?"

"No. They seemed to be getting on well," Zamfira replied. "They were talking and smiling at each other."

"Has anyone from the village come by the camp since you arrived?"

"You mean besides the search party?" Zamfira asked, her mouth pursing in anger. Jason was sure the villagers hadn't been kind or respectful when they had searched the camp.

"Yes."

Zamfira shrugged. "Your boy was here."

"My boy?" Jason asked.

"The redheaded lad. He came on Tuesday, in the afternoon."

"Are you sure?"

"Of course I am. Ask him."

Jason looked down at his folded hands, thinking how to proceed, when a thin wail erupted from the ornate bed at the rear of the caravan. Zamfira stood and went to fetch the baby, who snuggled against her and fell back asleep. The child was around eight months old, his curling dark hair so like his mother's. He was beautiful.

"Is he your first?" Jason asked.

"Yes, but not the last," Zamfira said, grinning happily.

"How far along are you?" Jason asked.

"About three months. It's a girl this time," Zamfira said confidently.

"How do you know?"

"I can always tell. Just one of my gifts."

"Don't you need a crystal ball?" Jason asked, somewhat unkindly.

"No. I sense things. Always have, since I was a girl." She looked at him intently. "This time, it will last," Zamfira suddenly said.

"Sorry?"

"She loves you and she'll be true."

"And you know this just by looking at me?" Jason asked, taken aback by Zamfira's unsolicited prediction.

"I know lots of things," Zamfira replied, a smile tugging at the corners of her generous mouth.

"But not who killed Imogen Chadwick or what happened to Moll Brody?"

"No, not that."

"Well, thanks anyway," Jason said.

He left the caravan, glad to get out into the sunshine. Zamfira had made him feel unsettled and strangely vulnerable. Jason walked across the meadow toward the dogcart, where Daniel was waiting for him, leaning against the conveyance and looking crestfallen.

"Were you able to learn anything useful?" Daniel asked once they were out of earshot of the camp.

"Zamfira saw Moll with a man on Tuesday. And it seems Micah has been by."

"Micah came to the camp? When?" Daniel asked.

"Tuesday afternoon."

"I think you'd best speak to him. I'll drop you off and then call on the Chadwicks."

"Have you spoken to Squire Talbot or his wife?' Jason asked.

Daniel shook his head. "Sarah and I will pay a condolence call within the next few days, but speaking to the Talbots is not a priority right now. Imogen hadn't lived with them since early March."

"Perhaps I should pay a condolence call," Jason suggested. "It's the neighborly thing to do."

"What a very good idea," Daniel agreed.

Chapter 12

Daniel presented himself at Chadwick Manor at eleven, as instructed. This time, Llewellyn was almost civil and escorted him directly to the drawing room, where the family was gathered, looking somber. The house was decked out for mourning. There was a black bow on the front door, the mirrors and windows were swathed in black crepe, and the clocks had been stopped at the approximate time of Imogen's death. The family wore unrelieved black, down to the cravat at Harry Chadwick's throat. Gas lamps were lit, making it feel like evening when in fact it wasn't yet noon.

"Please accept my deepest sympathies for your loss," Daniel said, looking from one Chadwick to another and hoping he would at least be invited to sit while he conducted his interviews.

"Thank you, Inspector," Harry Chadwick said. He looked pale and drawn, his stance rigid beside the unlit fireplace.

Caroline Chadwick occupied one settee, while her daughters sat across from her on a matching seat, their eyes red-rimmed, their faces deathly pale against the black of their gowns. A fair-haired man, presumably Sir Lawrence, sat in a wingchair, his legs crossed. He didn't wear black, but there was a black armband tied over the sleeve of his charcoal-gray morning coat.

"Please sit down, Inspector Haze," Caroline Chadwick said, finally remembering her manners. "May I present Sir Lawrence Foxley."

"Sir Lawrence." Daniel gave the man a curt nod, sat down in the second wingchair, and pulled out his notepad and pencil. "If it's all right, I would like to speak to each member of the family individually," Daniel said, looking to Caroline rather than Harry.

"We have nothing to hide from each other," Harry snapped.

"Now, Harry dear, Inspector Haze is only doing his job," Caroline said in a soothing tone. "It is our duty to cooperate. For Imogen's sake."

Harry gave an infinitesimal nod and turned away to stare toward the crepe-covered window.

"Whom shall you interview first?" Caroline asked.

"Mr. Chadwick, I'd like to start with you," Daniel replied.

"We'll be in the withdrawing room," Caroline announced, and gestured for her daughters to follow her.

Sir Lawrence heaved himself to his feet and joined the ladies, but not before clapping Harry on the shoulder in a silent gesture of support.

Once they were alone, Harry Chadwick took the chair Sir Lawrence had vacated. "Go on, then," he said belligerently.

"Mr. Chadwick," Daniel began, but Harry interrupted him.

"This is all your fault, you know, for allowing those people to squat on the land. They have no right to be there. No right whatsoever. I don't know why you're bothering with this sham of an investigation. They killed her. That's obvious to anyone who's not a complete imbecile. You should arrest the lot of them," Harry said hotly.

"And what reason would the Romani have to kill your wife?" Daniel asked.

"Well, I don't know," Harry sputtered. "What reason do they have for anything they choose to do?"

"I have no doubt they have their reasons for the things they do, Mr. Chadwick, like most people. In case of a murder, there's usually a motive, which I'm trying to establish. Now, if you don't mind," Daniel said, his pencil poised above a clean page. "When was the last time you saw your wife?"

"Tuesday afternoon, around two. She said she had a headache and went to her room. She wasn't planning to come down for dinner."

"Did you check on her at all after she retired?" Daniel asked.

"No. She asked not to be disturbed."

"Was Mrs. Chadwick upset or frightened in the days preceding her death?"

"Not that I noticed."

"Had she said anything unusual?" Daniel persisted.

"Imogen wasn't much of a talker," Harry said, surprising Daniel with the disdain he seemed to feel for his bride. "She had always been dull, but she became even more boring once we married."

"Did you regret the marriage?" Daniel asked carefully.

Harry shrugged. "I always knew I would marry Imogen. Our parents arranged it all years ago. But I did have a choice, as did she. So, no, I didn't regret the marriage."

"Were you faithful to her, Mr. Chadwick?"

Harry's cheeks flushed scarlet. "How dare you? Who do you think you are to ask me such questions?"

"I'm an inspector with the Brentwood Police Constabulary, Mr. Chadwick. Now, please answer the question."

Harry looked away, the answer written in his defensive posture. "No, I was not faithful to her, but I didn't keep a mistress, if that's what you're implying. I availed myself from time to time, when I felt the urge."

"And where did you find these girls?"

"Brentwood, London, wherever I happened to be at the time."

"Were you ever intimate with Moll Brody?" Daniel asked.

Harry looked genuinely surprised by the question. "Moll Brody? No, never. My grandfather gave me a piece of advice about women, Inspector, which I have found quite useful. 'Don't shit where you eat, Harry, my boy,' he said. I might not have loved Imogen, but I had no desire to humiliate her or make life uncomfortable for our future children."

Daniel nodded. The advice was crude but effective. Too many men became careless, an oversight that usually resulted in vicious gossip and a very unhappy home life with a woman who felt humiliated and betrayed.

"Did your wife know you weren't faithful to her?" Daniel asked.

"She suspected. She didn't mind," Harry said, glaring at Daniel. "She was happy not to have me in her bed."

"I believe she was with child," Daniel said gently.

Harry nodded. "She was pleased. It meant I wouldn't be troubling her with my tiresome husbandly demands for close to a year."

"Were you pleased?" Daniel asked.

"Yes, of course. That's the whole point of marriage, isn't it? To sire an heir."

"Mr. Chadwick, can you think of anyone who might have wanted to harm your wife? Anyone at all?"

Harry looked thoughtful for a moment. "No, I honestly can't. Imogen wasn't the type of person to inspire strong feelings in anyone. And you'd have to have strong feelings to garrote someone, wouldn't you?"

"Yes, you would," Daniel agreed.

"I am sorry she's dead, Inspector," Harry said, and for the first time, Daniel saw a glimmer of grief in his dark eyes.

"Thank you for your candor. Now, if you could please send in Sir Lawrence."

Chapter 13

Sir Lawrence smiled apologetically as he took a seat. "I'm afraid I didn't bring any mourning clothes. It's dreadful what happened. Just dreadful. If there's anything I can do to help. Anything at all," he said, his eyes narrowed as he studied Daniel.

Daniel studied him back. Sir Lawrence was in his mid to late twenties, and obviously took pains to stay fit. His suit was impeccably tailored, his hair artfully tousled. He wore a cabochon ruby on the pinky of his left hand, and a diamond tie pin glittered among the silk folds of his puff tie. His features were too blunt to be considered handsome, but on the whole, Sir Lawrence was what Daniel's mother would have called "a fine figure of a man." He had a presence and a certain charm. Daniel didn't know much about the man's character, but somehow, he thought he'd make a perfect husband for spoiled, haughty Lucinda.

"That's a very kind offer," Daniel said, suddenly realizing that the man was still awaiting a reply. "Tell me, Sir Lawrence, when did you arrive?"

"I arrived on Sunday afternoon, just before tea. I set off from London right after church," he added, giving Daniel a pious smile.

"I see. And how did you find the family when you got here?"

"In both good health and spirits. The country air is so bracing after the smoke-filled haze that passes for breathable air in London."

"When was the last time you saw Imogen Chadwick?" Daniel asked.

"Tuesday, lunch. I went out for a walk afterward, and by the time I returned, she had gone up to her room."

"Did you go out by yourself?"

"No, Lucinda came with me. And her maid," Sir Lawrence added swiftly.

"Where did you walk?"

"We took a few turns about the garden. All very proper, you understand," Sir Lawrence said, rolling his eyes.

"Did you see or hear anything unusual since your arrival?" Daniel asked, unsure what more to ask the man.

Sir Lawrence made a show of thinking. "I didn't, but then again, this was the first time I'd spent more than a few hours with the Chadwicks, so I wouldn't know what was unusual, would I? Am I free to go, Inspector?"

"Yes. Thank you, sir."

"Happy to help," Sir Lawrence said.

"Just one more question, Sir Lawrence," Daniel said. "The chap who became betrothed to Arabella was a friend of yours?"

If Sir Lawrence was surprised by the question, he didn't let on. "Yes, Mr. Gareth Butler, but we haven't spoken since he broke things off with Arabella. What he did was in poor taste, Inspector," Sir Lawrence said hotly.

"Why did Mr. Butler end the engagement?"

"Gareth found a more appealing prospect. The lady in question had refused his proposal several months before but seemed to change her mind once he was no longer available. It didn't take much for her to reel Gareth back in, since he'd held her in great esteem. They are to be married this summer. I'll send in Lucinda, shall I?" he asked, clearly tired of answering questions.

"Please."

Chapter 14

Lucinda settled on the settee, primly clasping her hands in her lap. Despite the black gown, she was still beautiful, her dark curls artfully arranged around her face and her startling blue eyes downcast as she waited for Daniel to begin. He wasn't fooled by her demure manner. Lucinda Chadwick was a hellion, a female version of Colonel Chadwick, who had been domineering, unforgiving, and sly.

"How can I help, Inspector?" Lucinda asked, raising her eyes to meet his probing gaze.

"When was the last time you saw Imogen?" Daniel asked.

"Tuesday lunch. Lawrence and I went for a walk after. I'm sure he already told you that."

"Yes, he did. Did you see anything while you were out walking?"

"Such as?" Lucinda challenged him.

"Such as Imogen heading toward the Gypsy camp," Daniel clarified.

Lucinda shook her head. "I didn't see anyone."

"Why would Imogen lie about not feeling well and sneak out to see the Gypsies?" Daniel asked, hoping Imogen might have confided in Lucinda.

Lucinda shrugged, making her curls dance. "Perhaps she needed hope."

"How do you mean?" Daniel asked, surprised by Lucinda's take on the situation.

"Imogen wasn't happy, Inspector. My brother is not exactly a loving husband, and Imogen was lonely and homesick."

"But her parents live right here in Birch Hill."

"Yes, they do, but she could no longer reside with them, being married," Lucinda explained patiently. "Her mother doted on her, and her father was happy to fulfill her every whim. I don't think she ever truly felt at home here."

"I see. And you think she went to have her fortune told to hear something that would make her believe things would change?"

"I do."

"Have you ever had your fortune told, Lucinda?" Daniel asked, using her Christian name without being invited to.

Lucinda smiled contemptuously. "I believe in making my own fortune, Inspector Haze. I don't need some dirty Gypsy to tell me that I will meet a tall, dark stranger. I prefer fair-haired men anyhow."

"I expect your wedding will have to be postponed," Daniel observed.

Lucinda sighed impatiently, as if Imogen's death were a huge inconvenience. "Not if I can help it."

"There is the mourning period to be observed," Daniel pointed out.

"There are ways to bring forth a wedding," Lucinda snapped, and instantly looked contrite.

Daniel remained silent, waiting to see what she would say next. Lucinda was brash, but he didn't think she'd be foolish enough to lie with Sir Lawrence before the wedding. He was too big a prize to risk losing, and a girl who was easily seduced could be just as easily discarded. Lucinda was too clever to give away the only thing of value she had to bring to a husband, besides her immense fortune. Unless she had already given it away to someone else and would simply play the virgin on her wedding night. Daniel wouldn't put it past her, but he didn't think Lucinda's purity had any bearing on the case, at least not at this stage of the investigation.

"I will respect whatever decision my mother and Sir Lawrence make," Lucinda said, raising her chin defiantly. "And, of course, I will mourn poor Imogen. She was like a sister to me."

"Was she?" Daniel asked. He didn't think Lucinda and Imogen had been particularly close, but having observed them together only at church and during the village fetes, he had little evidence to base this conclusion on.

"I'd known her all my life and always knew she'd marry Harry," Lucinda said. "But she was closer to Arabella. They were just more alike in temperament."

"Thank you, Lucinda. Now, please ask your sister to come in."

"Of course," Lucinda replied. Now that he was finished with her, she looked more relaxed, a small smile playing about her lips. "Good day to you, Inspector, and I hope you catch whoever did this awful thing or I shall never feel safe again." The words were innocent enough, but Daniel suspected she was making fun of him.

"Have no fear. The culprit will be apprehended," he said calmly, refusing to give her the satisfaction of betraying any uncertainty about his ability to bring the murderer to justice.

Chapter 15

Arabella Chadwick delicately dabbed at her eyes with a lace-trimmed handkerchief as she sat down on the settee. She was as pale as chalk, but her nose was red from constant wiping. Her eyes swam with tears as she lifted her gaze to meet Daniel's.

"When was the last time you saw Imogen, Miss Chadwick?" Daniel asked.

Arabella sniffled. "Around two on Tuesday afternoon. She didn't feel well and went to lie down."

"And what did you do after luncheon on Tuesday?"

"I went to the folly. I like to read there. I read until teatime."

"The folly?" Daniel asked. He wasn't aware there was a folly on the estate, but then why would he be?

"My father had it built for my mother, but she's not fond of it. She finds it too secluded. I'm the only one who goes there."

"You don't find it secluded?" Daniel asked.

"I do. That's why I like it. No one bothers me there. And there's a view of the lake, so it's pretty, especially in the autumn, when the leaves start to change."

"Did you see anyone while you were reading at the folly?"

"I saw Sir Lawrence and Lucinda walking in the garden. They went in around three."

"And what were you reading?" Daniel asked.

"*The Last Chronicle of Barset* by Anthony Trollope," Arabella replied. "Sir Lawrence brought a copy with him from London. He knew I was waiting for the final installment. It was very kind of him."

"Indeed," Daniel agreed. "Did you see Imogen sneak out of the house, Miss Chadwick?"

"No. The folly is on the west side of the estate, but the Romani campground is to the east. Imogen would have gone that way."

"Have you ever had your fortune told, Miss Chadwick?" Daniel asked.

Arabella blushed violently and nodded. "Once. The year before last."

"Did you go alone?"

"No. I had my maid with me."

"And did you feel at all threatened by the Romani while you were there?"

"No. They were nice."

"Why do you think Imogen wanted to have her fortune told?" Daniel asked.

"I think she wanted reassurance that she'd live a long and happy life," Arabella said.

"Because she was unhappy?"

"Because she was afraid to die in childbirth," Arabella replied in a half-whisper. "So many women do."

"I see. And did Imogen have any friends she might have met with after she left the grounds, someone who might have accompanied her to the Romani camp?"

"No. Lucinda and I were her only friends, but Imogen and Lucinda didn't really get on that well. Lucinda was always needling her, making her feel inadequate."

"So, you were her only confidante?" Daniel asked.

"Yes," Arabella added sadly. "She was my only real friend." Arabella stifled a sob as she hunched over, lost in her grief.

Daniel could certainly understand what had drawn the two young women together. They were both quiet and shy, the type of women who'd rather read a book or take a walk in the garden than attend a ball or ride in Rotten Row in the hopes of attracting some young buck's attention. Imogen might not have been happy in her marriage, but Daniel was certain she'd been relieved to be spared a London Season and the unrelenting pressure to find a suitable husband on her first outing into society. Just as he could imagine Arabella's dread at having to endure a second round without her sister.

"Is there anything else you would like to add?" Daniel asked desperately. He hadn't learned anything vital, and he so badly needed a clue.

Arabella shook her head. "I'm sorry, but there isn't much to tell."

"Thank you," Daniel said, and watched as Arabella slowly rose to her feet and walked toward the withdrawing room, her head bowed.

"Miss Chadwick," he called after her.

"Yes?"

"I'd like to speak to Imogen's maid."

Arabella nodded and disappeared through the door. Servants knew everything, and Imogen Chadwick's maid might have even been in on her plan to sneak out on Tuesday.

Chapter 16

A young woman of about twenty entered the room a few minutes later, accompanied by Caroline Chadwick.

"Inspector Haze, this is Hetty Pruitt. She was Imogen's maidservant." Caroline looked like she was about to settle on the settee, an intrusion Daniel could not allow.

"I need to speak to Miss Pruitt alone, please," Daniel said. Was Caroline afraid Hetty would reveal something about the family that Caroline didn't wish known? Daniel thought he'd already seen all their dirty linen during the investigation into Alexander McDougal's death, but perhaps there was more.

"Of course," Caroline said, and turned to leave the room, but not before giving Hetty a withering look. The maid looked like she was about to faint.

"Please, have a seat," Daniel invited once the door closed behind Caroline.

Hetty perched on the edge of the settee as if afraid to soil it.

"How long have you worked for the Chadwicks, Hetty?"

"Since March, sir. I came to Chadwick Manor with my mistress when she married Master Harry."

"And how long had you worked for the Talbots before that?"

"Since I were fifteen, sir. I started as an upstairs maid, but Mistress Imogen asked for me in particular when 'er first maid left to get married. She thought we'd get on, and we did."

"And did your mistress share confidences with you?" Daniel asked softly. He didn't want to spook Hetty more than she already was, but given that Hetty and Imogen had been around the same age and had known each other for years, it was possible that Imogen had been more forthcoming with her maid than she was with Arabella and Lucinda, who were the sisters of her future spouse and would have divided loyalties, at best.

"Sometimes," Hetty mumbled.

"Did you know Imogen planned to visit the Gypsy campsite?" Daniel asked.

Hetty seemed to draw in on herself, as if she were about to be struck, but did not reply.

"Hetty, I'm not going to tell anyone what you said. Our interview is confidential."

"Mrs. Chadwick will never find out what I said?" she asked, desperate for confirmation. "Ye promise, Inspector?"

"You have my word."

Hetty nodded. "Yes, I knew she were planning to go."

"Did you help her leave the house without being detected?"

"I told her when no one were about, and it were safe to leave 'er room."

"But you didn't go with her?" Daniel asked.

"No. She wished to go alone."

"Did your mistress sneak out often?" Daniel inquired.

Hetty's expression was as sour as if she'd just sucked on a lemon. She was afraid to tell Daniel the truth, and he could hardly blame her. If Caroline Chadwick found out, Hetty would be dismissed without a character reference. In a world where discretion was everything, the lack of references could spell the difference between a life of relative comfort and near starvation. But Daniel needed to know.

"Hetty?" he prompted.

"Mistress Imogen sneaked out from time to time, but not so much anymore."

"Where did she go?"

"To see Mr. Reed," Hetty replied, her voice barely audible.

"And who's Mr. Reed?" Daniel asked. He'd never heard the name before.

"Mr. Reed is Squire Talbot's estate agent. Mistress Imogen fancied herself in love with him."

"Did Mr. Reed return her feelings?"

"I don't rightly know, sir. I were never with them when they met."

"And did you help to facilitate these meetings?" Daniel asked. Hetty nodded.

"Did your mistress believe there might have been a future for them?"

"She never said, but I think she dreamed of it, sir." Hetty looked at the door with longing, but Daniel wasn't finished with her yet.

"Could the child have been Mr. Reed's, Hetty?"

Hetty shook her head. "It weren't like that between them."

"I thought you didn't know how it was," Daniel pointed out.

"I'd know if she'd lain with Mr. Reed. A maid always knows these things, sir."

Daniel studied her. "How would you have known?"

Hetty flushed scarlet. "I'd see it when I washed her unmentionables. There'd be stains. And there's a smell." Daniel could barely hear the last word but could guess at what she was alluding to. "Mistress Imogen were a maid on her wedding night, sir. There was evidence."

Daniel nodded. "Hetty, was your mistress hoping to run away with Mr. Reed?"

"If she were, it never 'appened," Hetty replied. "May I go now, sir? I 'ave chores to be getting on with."

"Certainly. Just a few more questions, though. Did Squire Talbot know of his daughter's interest in the estate agent?"

"No, sir. No one knew."

"Where did they meet?"

"In Bloody Mead."

"Right. Thank you, Hetty," Daniel said, and closed his notebook.

"Ye promised," Hetty reminded him as she stood to leave.

"And I will keep my promise. Nothing you said to me will ever leave this room," Daniel said, and meant it. He'd do everything possible to protect Hetty from Caroline Chadwick's wrath, if it came to that.

Caroline swept into the room as soon as Hetty left. "Well, Inspector? Was Hetty able to shed any light?" she asked, watching him like a hawk whose talons were about to rip into his face.

"Sadly, no. She doesn't know anything."

Caroline nodded. "I didn't think she did. She's such a timid little thing. Almost as timid as Imogen was. They were a perfect match."

"Will you keep Hetty Pruitt on now that her mistress is gone?" Daniel asked, irrationally worried about the maid.

"Yes. She's a good worker, and there's always work to be done in a house this size," she said.

"I thank you for your time and patience," Daniel said, ready to take his leave.

"Anything we can do to help. Have you learned anything that might identify Imogen's killer?" she asked pointedly.

"No, I don't believe I have."

Caroline scoffed. "That's because you're looking in the wrong place. That's the problem with the police. They always seem to discount the obvious."

"And what would that be, Mrs. Chadwick?"

"That the Gypsies killed her," Caroline snarled. "And the sooner you arrest them, the better for all involved."

"I will certainly take your advice under consideration. Good day, madam."

Daniel left the house and walked toward the stable yard, wondering if Caroline Chadwick might actually have a point.

Chapter 17

After interviewing the Chadwicks, Daniel decided to stop by the Talbot estate to speak to Mr. Reed. How was it that he'd never met the man? In a place like Birch Hill, everyone knew everyone else, even if only in passing. St. Catherine's was the social hub of the village, where the young and the old, the rich and the poor came together, not only to worship God but also to gossip, attend village fetes, and bury their dead. And just across the green was the Red Stag. There wasn't a man in Birch Hill who hadn't stopped in to enjoy a jar of ale with his mates. Even the likes of Squire Talbot and Harry Chadwick had been known to drink at the tavern. But Daniel had never met Mr. Reed, not even in passing.

After asking several helpful farm hands, Daniel found the elusive Mr. Reed, or Mr. James, as the workers called him, in an office just off the stable block. The door was open, so he walked in and was greeted by a friendly smile.

"Well, hello. May I help you, sir?" the man asked.

"Are you James Reed?"

"At your service," the man said, still smiling.

Daniel didn't consider himself a competent judge of male beauty, but even he could see that Mr. Reed was extraordinarily handsome. With thickly lashed green eyes, wavy hair in a rich sable brown, and full, sensuous lips, the man looked like a romantic hero from the type of novels Sarah used to enjoy before they were married. Deeply embarrassed by this rogue thought, Daniel cleared his throat and introduced himself, hoping the man hadn't noticed his discomfiture.

"I am Inspector Haze of the Brentwood Constabulary. I'd like a word."

"Of course. Is this about the murder?" James Reed asked, his gaze instantly turning somber. "Please." He indicated the visitor chair. "I'm afraid I don't have any refreshments to offer you."

"That's quite all right," Daniel said as he took the proffered seat, although a cup of tea would have been most welcome just then. He was parched.

"How can I help?" Reed asked. He moved aside a pile of receipts and closed the ledger he'd been working on, folding his hands on top and fixing his gaze on Daniel. He looked earnest and eager to be of assistance.

"Mr. Reed, how is it that you and I have never met?" Daniel asked, needing to put his curiosity to rest. "This is a small village, and yet this is the first time I've heard your name, much less had the pleasure of seeing you in person."

"Oh, that's simple," James Reed replied, smiling apologetically. "Part of my arrangement with the squire is that I get room and board."

"You reside at the house?" Daniel asked, surprised that an estate agent would be treated like a member of the family.

"Well, yes, but I have a room in the servants' wing. I take my meals in my room, since I'm neither a servant nor a member of the family."

"That must be awkward."

"I don't mind, as long as I don't have to travel back and forth every day."

"Travel where?"

"I have an elderly mother who lives in Brentwood. I visit her on my days off, which is why you have never seen me at St. Catherine's or in the village in general."

"You've never visited the tavern?" Daniel asked, incredulous.

"I don't imbibe alcohol. It doesn't agree with me," James Reed said. "I'm happier with a cup of tea."

"I see. And how long have you worked for the squire?"

"Nearly six years now."

"Can you tell me about your relationship with Imogen Chadwick?" Daniel asked, and was gratified to see a pained look on the man's handsome face.

"I have known Miss Imogen since she was thirteen," James Reed began. "She was a shy, quiet girl who was often solitary. When she turned sixteen, Squire Talbot surprised her with a horse for her birthday. She named her Queenie," he said.

"Sorry, but what does this have to do with your eh…friendship?" Daniel asked.

"I'm getting to that," James Reed replied patiently. "As you can see, my office is near the stables, so I would often see Miss Imogen going for a ride, or simply visiting Queenie. When she did, she sometimes stopped in to say hello, and we would chat for a few minutes. Over time, I began to realize that the reason she visited the stables so frequently was because she needed an excuse to see me. She had developed romantic feelings toward me."

"And did you return those feelings, Mr. Reed?" Daniel asked, hoping he sounded understanding rather than judgmental.

"I thought she was a pleasant young woman, that's all."

"Did either of you ever address the issue?"

James Reed colored, his reaction making Daniel lean forward in his eagerness to hear what the man had to say.

"Unfortunately, yes. It was about a month before her wedding. Miss Imogen came to my office. She seemed agitated, and her color was high."

"What happened?" Daniel asked.

"Imogen was nervous, tripping over her words when she spoke, but she finally told me what was on her mind. She said her father had been giving her a small allowance since she turned twelve, just so she would have a little money of her own should she wish to buy a trinket or a gift for someone. She had saved nearly two hundred pounds since she hardly spent any of that money."

"That's quite a sum," Daniel said. "What did she propose to do with it?"

"She said the money would last us a few years if we were careful. She suggested we board a train in Brentwood and go north, eventually making our way to Gretna Green, where we would be married. Once wed, she thought we could settle in Scotland and lie low until the scandal died down."

Daniel looked closely at the man, trying to assess the veracity of his account. The Imogen Talbot he'd known before her marriage would never have had the courage to suggest such a plan, but then again, given her less-than-loving relationship with Harry, he could see how she might have been desperate to try to alter her fate.

"What did you say to her?" Daniel asked.

"I told her that I held her in great esteem, but I didn't share her dreams for the future and could not accept her proposal."

"How did she react?"

James Reed looked unbearably sad. "She was hurt and humiliated. Crushed," he added. "I think she really thought it was possible."

"Would you have taken her up on her offer had you had feelings for her?" Daniel inquired, curious what the man would say.

"No, Inspector. If I did, I'd never be able to find respectable employment to support my family. Squire Talbot would hunt us down to the ends of the earth, and Gretna Green would be the first place he'd look. He'd have the marriage annulled and make sure to ruin me so thoroughly I'd regret having ever been born. No woman is worth that."

"And did you see Miss Imogen after that fateful conversation?"

"She left in tears, and our paths did not cross again. It's easy to avoid each other in a house that size."

"Surely you've seen her since," Daniel insisted.

"I saw her drive up to the house with her husband once they returned from their wedding trip. And then I thought I saw her again when I went for a walk in the woods, but I was mistaken."

"Whom *did* you see?" Daniel asked.

"I mistook Arabella Chadwick for Imogen. From a distance, they look somewhat alike, particularly if their hair is covered by a bonnet."

"Was Arabella Chadwick walking in the woods?" Daniel asked.

"I saw her reading in the folly. It's a favorite place of hers," James Reed said, and instantly looked like he regretted the words.

"How would you know that, Mr. Reed?"

"Because the path I like to walk takes me past the Chadwick estate, and I sometimes see her there."

"And Imogen Chadwick? You never saw her out walking or riding?"

"No. I thought I would because Imogen liked to ride."

Daniel decided not to share unnecessarily personal information with James Reed, but he thought Imogen might not have been riding to safeguard the pregnancy. Dr. Parsons would surely have advised against it.

"Mr. Reed, can you think of anyone who would wish to hurt Imogen Chadwick?" Daniel asked.

James Reed shook his head. "Just because I didn't love her doesn't mean I didn't like her, Inspector. She was a kind, caring person. I can't imagine that anyone would intentionally wish to harm her. Are you sure her death wasn't an accident?" he asked, his eyes lighting with hope.

"I'm quite sure, Mr. Reed. Thank you for your candor."

"I hope you catch whoever did this, Inspector Haze. They deserve to swing."

"You won't hear an argument from me, Mr. Reed. Goodbye."

Daniel walked out into the sunshine and mounted the dogcart. Perhaps he should have asked James Reed about Moll, but if the man never went into the Red Stag, chances were their paths had never crossed. As far as Daniel knew, the only time Moll had visited the Talbot estate was for the annual Christmas ball to which Squire Talbot invited the whole village, but Daniel couldn't recall ever seeing James Reed at the party. Perhaps he preferred to spend the evening with his mother, or maybe he'd chosen not to attend to avoid the daughter of the house.

Chapter 18

Jason waited until the socially appropriate hour of one o'clock to pay a call on the Talbots. Had they been in London, he would have had to wait for their At Home day to visit and might have been among a number of visitors, but the rules were slightly less stringent in the country, which he was grateful for. He was still learning the myriad restrictions that governed British society and wasn't sure that the same applied for mourning calls. As plain Mr. Redmond, he'd be cut no slack, but as Lord Redmond, he was given some leeway, and his American cluelessness was viewed as charming, at least until he turned his back.

Jason thought he might have a talk with Micah while he waited, but Micah and Mr. Sullivan had gone out, taking their painting supplies with them. Mr. Sullivan had Micah paint at least one morning per week. Micah wasn't what one would call a gifted artist, but he painted from the heart and often drew scenes of battle or images of fallen men. Shawn Sullivan referred to it as the art cure and thought this form of expression would help Micah come to terms with the awful things he'd seen during the American Civil War and the personal losses he'd suffered.

Micah did seem happier, but Jason wasn't sure if it was due to the painting or the fact that he'd been reunited with Mary. He thought the latter but didn't discourage the art lessons. They certainly couldn't hurt. He'd speak to Micah later on, maybe before tea, when Micah had free time to either roam the countryside with Tom Marin or curl up with a book, his decision influenced by the weather.

Jason asked for the curricle to be brought around. He didn't relish making a condolence call, but he did enjoy driving through the countryside in the luxurious vehicle. His grandfather, God rest his soul, had enjoyed the finer things, and the curricle had been one of his last indulgences before his death. Giles Redmond had likely never imagined that the grandson he'd never met would be the one driving it after he was gone.

Having surrendered the conveyance to a groom, Jason approached the front door and knocked, his hand brushing against the black bow fastened to the door just above the knocker. He hoped he wasn't intruding on the Talbots in their grief. The butler, Bingham, showed him into the drawing room, where Mrs. Talbot sat hunched on a settee, her gaze fixed on an oriental vase positioned on a small table between two windows. The room was dim and stuffy, the windows closed and adorned with black crepe. She seemed to rouse herself when Bingham announced Jason, and tried valiantly to rearrange her features into an expression of welcome. The result was more a grimace of pain that nearly broke Jason's heart.

"Lord Redmond, how kind of you to call. I'm afraid the squire is not here. He finds it easier to keep busy," she said, her voice faltering.

She looked so lost, Jason wished he could take her in his arms and hold her while she wept, but Mrs. Talbot's eyes were bone-dry despite her grief. Perhaps she hadn't reached the stage where she could cry and release the flood of emotions she had to be feeling.

"Mrs. Talbot, if there's anything I can do," Jason said as he settled across from her. He suddenly realized that he didn't know her Christian name. He'd always thought of her as the squire's wife or Mrs. Talbot. He supposed he had viewed Imogen in the same way, through the lens of those she was related to.

"You're very kind, your lordship," Mrs. Talbot said. "I wish there was something to be done. Even to plan a funeral would give me something to occupy my mind and my time, but everything will be taken care of by the Chadwicks, so all I can do is sit here and think of my darling Immy and the wonderful daughter she was."

"She was a lovely young woman," Jason said. "Did she confide in you at all?" he asked and felt like an absolute cad for questioning a grieving woman.

"Not recently," Mrs. Talbot said softly. "I had lost her trust."

"Why would you think that?"

"It's my fault she's dead, Lord Redmond," Mrs. Talbot said vehemently. She was twisting her hands in her lap, her gaze agitated as she looked at him, her expression pleading for understanding.

"How do you mean, Mrs. Talbot?"

"It's all my fault," the woman repeated. "I should have listened to her. I should have been more understanding."

She was growing more upset, and Jason wondered if she was in the grip of hysteria. Perhaps she needed a tonic to calm her nerves, but he could hardly suggest it. The Talbots saw Dr. Parsons, who was the only physician in the village as far as they were concerned. The English didn't see a surgeon as a proper doctor, since surgeons didn't usually attend university but were apprenticed instead. Surgery was on par with butchery, and a surgeon was not granted the title of Doctor but referred to as Mister. Jason was university educated and had years of hands-on experience, but now was not the time to point that out.

"Mrs. Talbot, perhaps you should summon Dr. Parsons," Jason suggested gently when bright spots of color appeared on her pale cheeks.

The woman shook her head stubbornly. "I don't need to be sedated. I need to feel this pain and know that I'm doing penance for the wrong I've done."

"And what wrong is that?" Jason asked gently.

"Immy came to me. Just before Christmas. She begged me to speak to the squire. She wanted to break off the engagement to Harry Chadwick. She didn't love him, she said, and she couldn't imagine spending the rest of her life with him. She called him callous and shallow," Mrs. Talbot added through a sob.

"And what did you say to her?" Jason asked, although the answer was obvious.

"I told her not to be a silly girl and to put her trust in her father, who knew what was best for her. I dismissed her feelings and told her never to speak of breaking the engagement again for fear of word reaching the Chadwicks. I should have listened to her, should have at least tried to understand what she was going through, but I was afraid."

Mrs. Talbot took a shuddering breath and continued. "Imogen wasn't the type of girl who'd have done well during a London Season. She'd have hated being paraded and appraised as if she were a horse. She knew Harry. She was comfortable with him. And who was to say that any other man who was interested in her wouldn't be as shallow and callous as Harry Chadwick? At least married to Harry, she'd be close to us, and not halfway across the country, where we might see her once a year if we were lucky enough to be invited. Few men relish the company of their in-laws." Mrs. Talbot dabbed at her eyes and wiped her nose as delicately as she could.

"And a broken engagement can damage a girl's reputation. People start saying all kinds of terrible things," Mrs. Talbot added. "Just look at poor Arabella. She's a charming girl, and I'm sure it's not her fault her betrothed had a change of heart, but everyone blames her as if she'd done something to drive him away, or as if he'd discovered she wasn't worthy of being his wife." Mrs. Talbot was speaking fast, almost babbling, her nerves stretched to the breaking point. "It was my fault," she cried. "Immy died because I wouldn't listen to her."

"Mrs. Chadwick, Imogen sneaked out to have her fortune told and came upon someone who meant her harm. She didn't die because of anything you did or did not do."

"And why would she want to have her fortune told if not to be reassured that there was something good in the future? Perhaps she hoped to be told that she would be widowed. She'd be free of Harry then. Free to choose for herself." Mrs. Talbot clapped a hand over her mouth, as if realizing she'd said too much. "I'm sorry… I didn't mean… I shouldn't have…" The words came out tripping over each other, her distress mounting.

"Mrs. Talbot, if you send your maid back with me, I can give her a tincture of laudanum. A few drops mixed into a glass of water would help you to calm down. You need to get some rest. You're distraught."

"My daughter is dead," Mrs. Talbot cried shrilly. "Do you honestly believe a good night's sleep will change that?"

"Of course not, but you must look after yourself."

Mrs. Talbot looked at him with pity. "I appreciate your concern, my lord, but a woman has little to live for besides her children. Immy is gone, and Oliver has his own life now. He's happy in London and doesn't want to come back. I have nothing left. Nothing," she sobbed.

"You still have the squire," Jason suggested, and instantly regretted his words.

Mrs. Talbot glared at him as if he had just reminded her that she still had her pet canary. Knowing Squire Talbot, he didn't imagine the man paid much attention to the feelings of his wife. She was simply there, much like a chair or a painting he had admired at one time and acquired to add to his possessions. Jason could certainly understand why Imogen Talbot hadn't wanted to marry Harry. She had foreseen the same type of marriage her parents had and had wished for something better.

"I'll leave you to rest," Jason said. "If you change your mind about the tonic, just send your maid to collect it. No one has to know," he assured her.

"Thank you, Lord Redmond, but I will take my punishment as it comes," Mrs. Talbot said. "I deserve it, and if the guilt and grief kill me, so much the better."

"I'm sorry, Mrs. Talbot. I really am," Jason said, but she was no longer listening. Her gaze was fixed on the same spot as before, her hands clasped in her lap. Jason walked out of the drawing room to the foyer, where Bingham was already waiting with his hat and walking stick and escorted him to the door.

Chapter 19

Having paid a condolence call on the Talbots, Jason decided that it would only be right to pay one on the Chadwicks, as well. Daniel would have finished interviewing the family by now, so the coast should be clear.

When Jason presented himself at the door, Llewellyn looked sour as ever but didn't dare to turn him away. Caroline Chadwick was too much of a social climber to refuse a call from anyone with a title, even someone who was no longer a potential husband for one of her girls.

Stepping aside to let him in, Llewellyn waited patiently while Jason handed his things to a maid, then led him into the drawing room, announcing him in a hushed voice to show deference to the bereaved. To Jason's disappointment, there were only three people in the drawing room—Caroline Chadwick, Arabella, and Lucinda. He had hoped to meet Sir Lawrence and take his measure.

"Why, Lord Redmond, it's been too long," Caroline Chadwick said as she came forward to greet him, a wistful smile on her face. "Seems you only visit us when there's been a murder."

"I'm very sorry for your loss," Jason said, glancing at Arabella and Lucinda, whose eyes were downcast. Arabella looked grief-stricken, while Lucinda appeared bored, probably more than ready to get on with her life. It was more difficult to discern how their mother was handling the tragedy, since she worked harder to hide her true feelings.

The last time Jason had seen Caroline Chadwick, she'd worn a striped gown of navy blue and magenta with cream lace adorning the neckline and elbow-length sleeves, and had looked radiant, the gown serving to enhance her vivid coloring. Today, she wore unrelieved black, which made her fair skin appear almost translucent and her auburn hair shockingly bright. But she was an attractive woman regardless, and she knew it.

"Thank you, my lord. It's kind of you to call on us at this dreadful time. Imogen was like one of my own girls," Caroline said. "And she was like a sister to Arabella and Lucinda. Wasn't she, girls?"

Arabella and Lucinda nodded in unison, but neither said anything, leaving Caroline to fill the silence.

"Do sit down. Will you take some refreshment? I was about to ring for tea," Caroline said. Despite the mourning attire, she didn't behave like someone overcome with grief. If anything, her demeanor was more appropriate to a social call.

"Thank you. Tea would be lovely," Jason replied. He took a moment to study the girls more closely while Caroline rang for tea.

Arabella looked wan and a bit vacant. She was thinner than she had been. Jason couldn't help casting a professional eye over the girl but didn't see any outward signs of illness. The disappointment and embarrassment caused by her broken engagement must have taken their toll, and now she was mourning her lifelong friend. It was only natural that she would appear stricken.

Lucinda, on the other hand, had blossomed since he'd met her nearly a year ago. She had been lovely then, but still a child, a tomboy who liked to fence and tear around the countryside clad in a shirt and britches, to the great embarrassment of her mother. She was all woman now. Despite the black gown, she managed to look alluring. Her dark curls were lustrous and her skin like a fresh peach, dewy and delicate. She caught Jason looking at her and met his gaze head on, a small smile tugging her lips as she studied him in return. The look she gave him was not that of an innocent young girl; it was the look of a woman who knew what she was looking for in a man. She clearly found him attractive, a thought Jason recoiled from. What he knew of Lucinda Chadwick was enough to put him off forever.

Jason tore his gaze away, hoping Caroline hadn't noticed the exchange, but she was busy pouring out the tea that had just been brought in by a parlor maid. Caroline handed Jason a cup, and he accepted it gratefully, glad of something to occupy his hands. There was a plate of cucumber sandwiches and one of teacakes. Jason reached for a teacake. He still didn't get the point of cucumber sandwiches, which were tasteless, soggy, and stuck to the roof of one's mouth unless instantly washed down with tea.

"I hear you finally gave up on your silly refusal to use your title. Very wise of you, my lord. If you have it, use it, I always say," Caroline said, nodding in approval.

"I grew tired of correcting people," Jason said. It was difficult to explain to most English people why he preferred to use his army rank to his title, since one was so much more desirable than the other. How could he make them understand that he was much prouder of having been a captain in the Union Army than a nobleman? The title meant nothing to him, more so because he hadn't grown up with the knowledge that he would inherit a great estate.

Had Jason's father survived the train accident that had killed him and his wife, he would have inherited the title and the estate and might have rid himself of both before Jason was faced with making any life-altering decisions as the last surviving Redmond. It had been Jason's plan to sell off the estate and return home, but he'd found early on that he was in no rush to get back to the empty house in Washington Square, or the painful news of his ex-fiancé having married his best friend while Jason was in prison.

But the real reason Jason had decided to use the title was because of Katherine. He wanted her to enjoy all the respect that would come with her new role as Lady Redmond. She didn't care about such things, but Jason wanted to give her and their future children a social position to be proud of, even if they decided to settle in the States one day. As of now, he was in no rush. He was happy for the first time in years, and he meant to make the most of his new life.

"I hear you are to be congratulated," Caroline Chadwick said, interrupting his reverie. Jason and Katherine had been engaged since December, but this was the first time Caroline had acknowledged their upcoming marriage, despite having seen them several times since returning from London at the end of March. "How very American of you to follow your heart and marry for love," she said, making the put-down sound like a compliment. "Katherine is a lucky girl, indeed. And just think, once you're wed, we'll be related by marriage."

"Will we?" Jason asked, surprised.

"Of course. Katherine is second cousin to our dearly departed Imogen, so we'll be family."

"Indeed," Jason said, for lack of anything else to say. Being related to the Chadwicks was not something he aspired to.

"Really, Mother," Arabella said, clearly shocked that Caroline would attempt to profit from the relationship. "Is now really the time?"

"It's always the time," Lucinda said under her breath. "Leave it, Bella."

"We had our own happy news before this dreadful business," Caroline went on, blithely ignoring Arabella's comment and the impropriety of discussing Lucinda's engagement during a condolence call.

Imogen had died less than two days before, and already she'd been dismissed from Caroline's mind. Jason couldn't help wondering if anyone in this house truly mourned her. He thought Arabella would miss her company, but neither Caroline nor Lucinda appeared particularly afflicted, and he was sure Harry Chadwick wasn't in the throes of grief. If anything, he was probably relieved. With Imogen gone and Harry in possession of her handsome dowry, he would now be free to marry a woman of his choice, or more accurately, a woman his mother approved of but had not chosen for him. He was the master of Chadwick Manor and one of the wealthiest landowners in the county. He was also young, fit, and handsome. Once he was out of mourning, the world would spread before him like a buffet of opportunities, and Harry could sample the offerings at will before making a selection.

Perhaps Jason was judging the Chadwicks too harshly based on his previous experience of them, he thought ruefully.

They'd known Imogen her whole life. Surely they felt a sense of loss at her death and would grieve for her. Not even the Chadwicks could be so callous as to dismiss poor, pregnant Imogen without a second thought and get on with their lives as soon as the funeral was behind them.

"Sir Lawrence thinks it's only proper that we postpone the wedding," Caroline said, ignoring Arabella's outraged glare. "Being a baronet, he's so much more in tune with the rules of society. Of course, we wouldn't dream of celebrating so soon after Imogen's death. Would we, Lucinda?"

"Of course not, Mother," Lucinda muttered into her teacup.

If it were up to her, Jason was sure Caroline would only delay the wedding by a few months, but she would be harshly judged by society for not observing the mourning customs, and the decision would reflect poorly on Sir Lawrence and his reputation. Jason was sure Lucinda bridled at having to observe a year of mourning for a sister-in-law she probably hadn't given much thought to, but propriety had to be observed, regardless.

"Perhaps six months, since Imogen wasn't a direct relative of Lucinda's," Caroline continued. "A Christmas wedding can be charming. Don't you think, my lord?"

"Yes, charming," Jason agreed.

"It'd have to be tasteful and discreet, of course, but I think people will understand the desire of two young people to finally marry and get on with their lives. Sir Lawrence and Lucinda are so devoted to each other," she crooned, looking affectionately at Lucinda, who looked mutinous.

"What do you think, Lucinda? Won't a Christmas wedding be lovely?"

"Does it matter what I think?" Lucinda asked, sounding surprisingly defeated. "It will be whatever you decide. Isn't it always?"

"And where is Sir Lawrence?" Jason asked. "I was hoping to make his acquaintance." Normally, he wouldn't have broached the subject during a condolence call, but since Caroline had brought up the wedding, it seemed acceptable to inquire.

"He went for a ride with Harry. Young men find it so difficult to remain indoors, even in times of bereavement. Sir Lawrence resides in London for most of the year, so he misses the pleasures of the country. He has a charming house in Belgravia and a sizeable estate in Surrey," Caroline said, unable to resist singing the praises of her future son-in-law. "In fact, he's decided to redecorate his London residence and wanted Lucinda's input. So kind of him," she gushed. "He wishes to involve her in every step of the process, but she'll be happy with whatever he chooses. Won't you, Lucinda?"

"I do have my own opinions, Mother," Lucinda retorted. "I'd like to have some say in how my home looks."

"Sir Lawrence has excellent taste," Caroline replied warily.

Lucinda scoffed. "Nevertheless, I intend to be the mistress of my own house."

Caroline glared at Lucinda but didn't argue. "In fact, Sir Lawrence has invited us to visit his country estate once the newlyweds return from their wedding trip. We are greatly looking forward to it. Aren't we, Arabella?"

Arabella nodded miserably. Caroline's attempts at engaging her daughters in the conversation weren't going as she might have hoped.

"It's even more remote than Chadwick Manor," Lucinda said acidly.

"He does have many fine horses," Caroline reminded her wayward daughter.

Lucinda brightened somewhat. "I love horses. I'll spend all my free time riding."

"Riding is all well and good, but there are more genteel pursuits for a young lady, especially a young lady who is soon to marry a baronet."

"I'd rather die than take up embroidery or join some boring committee dedicated to good works," Lucinda grumbled.

"When is the funeral to be?" Jason asked, sensing an argument he had no wish to witness was about to break out.

"On Sunday, after the service. I've already spoken to Reverend Talbot, and he's agreed. Unfortunately, someone from the village is to be buried on Sunday as well, but they will just have to wait until we're finished or move their funeral service to Monday. Someone of Imogen's standing takes precedence over a farmer," Caroline added with obvious disdain.

Jason could understand Caroline Chadwick's desire to have the funeral done with as quickly as possible. It was unseasonably warm, and a body wouldn't keep for long, especially when all the windows were closed and the deceased was laid out in state in an open casket.

"I do hope you will do us the honor," Caroline was saying.

"Honor?" Jason had completely missed her last comment.

"Of attending the funeral. Imogen would have wanted you there," Caroline clarified.

I highly doubt Imogen would have cared, Jason thought, but inclined his head politely. "Of course. I would like to pay my respects to Mrs. Chadwick." Jason set down his empty cup. "I have imposed on you long enough. It's time I was going."

"Thank you, Lord Redmond. Spending this time with you has been a bright spot in what has otherwise been a very dismal day," Caroline said. "And do call again under happier circumstances. Promise me you will," she cajoled.

"Of course." Jason was just about to leave when Harry Chadwick and Sir Lawrence walked in.

"Sir Lawrence, allow me to present our close neighbor and dear friend, Lord Redmond," Caroline said. "Sir Lawrence Foxley."

Jason stood to greet the new arrivals. "Good day, gentlemen," he said, unsure if he was supposed to greet Sir

Lawrence first because of his rank. In either case, Jason thought he outranked a baronet, but wouldn't swear to it. The levels of nobility and the different forms of address were still a deep, dark mystery to him.

"My lord, it's a pleasure to meet you," Sir Lawrence said. Jason couldn't help noticing that he had the upright bearing of a soldier. The man's presence seemed to fill the room.

"Likewise," Jason replied, resuming his seat.

"I hear you're from America. How exciting. I have always wanted to visit the United States. You fought in the Civil War?" Sir Lawrence said, making Jason cringe inwardly. He had no wish to speak of his wartime experiences but couldn't be rude and refuse to answer the baronet's questions.

"Yes, I did."

"A captain in the Union Army, Harry told me. Imagine that," Sir Lawrence exclaimed. "And you're a surgeon."

"Lord Redmond assists the police," Harry said caustically. "He performs postmortems on victims of murder."

"Do you, indeed?" Sir Lawrence exclaimed. "How extraordinary. Why? If you don't mind my asking."

"Someone has to," Jason replied.

"Aw, come now, my good sir, surely there's more to it than that," Sir Lawrence said.

"Sir Lawrence, I don't think this is an appropriate conversation to be having in front of the ladies," Jason said. In fact, Arabella had grown even paler, her eyes wide with revulsion.

"I do apologize," Sir Lawrence said, looking at Arabella with concern. "Are you quite all right, Arabella?"

She nodded. "Yes, Sir Lawrence."

"Harry took me past the Gypsy camp," Sir Lawrence said, his eyes flashing with annoyance. "I don't allow them on my land."

"That meadow doesn't belong to the Chadwick estate," Harry said. "I have no authority to chase them off. Believe me, I would dearly love to be rid of them."

"If it were my estate, I'd see them off," Lucinda said hotly. "And they'd never come back. I'd make sure of that."

"Lucinda, for goodness sake!" Caroline cried.

"Oh, come on, Mother. You said the same thing yourself time and time again. And now that tavern wench is missing. I wager they killed her too."

"We don't know that," Jason protested.

"Don't we?" Lucinda demanded. "Where is she, then? They probably threw her body into the river or left it in the woods for the animals to feed on. I'm sure they enjoyed devouring her entrails," Lucinda announced. Jason was surprised to see that Sir Lawrence looked amused rather than appalled by her outburst.

Arabella let out a tiny sigh and slumped down on the settee. Caroline was next to her in moments, pushing a bottle of smelling salts beneath her nose, until Arabella came to with a start, her gaze wild and confused.

"Mrs. Chadwick, perhaps you should help Arabella to her room. She needs to rest," Jason said. *And loosen that tight corset*, he added inwardly.

"Yes. Of course," Caroline said, pulling Arabella to her feet. "Come, my dear."

"Allow me to help." Sir Lawrence put his arm around Arabella, but his gaze was fixed on Lucinda, who had a small smile playing about her lips. Jason was surprised to see a look of desire pass between them. Whatever this marriage was going to be, it wouldn't be boring, he decided.

"Well, I think that's my cue to leave," Jason said to no one in particular.

He followed Caroline Chadwick, Sir Lawrence, and Arabella from the room, collected his things, stepped out into the

May afternoon, and waited on the steps for the groom to bring around his curricle.

Chapter 20

When Jason returned home, all was peaceful and quiet, a rare occurrence these days.

"Where is everyone?" he asked Dodson as he surrendered his hat and walking stick.

"Taking tea in the garden. Will you join them, sir?"

"I don't think so."

To Dodson's great surprise, Jason crossed the foyer and disappeared through the green baize door that separated the servants' quarters from the rest of the house. He went down to the kitchen, where Mrs. Dodson was busy preparing dinner. She was fashioning some sort of mush into elongated tubes.

"What are you making, Mrs. D?" Jason asked as he took a seat at the scrubbed oak table.

Mrs. Dodson didn't look the least bit surprised. Unlike most masters, Jason often found his way to the kitchen, especially when there was something on his mind and he longed for someone to talk to. He would have loved to talk things over with Katherine, but calling at the vicarage would have to wait.

"Stuffed pork loin and potato croquettes," Mrs. Dodson replied.

Jason looked around. "Where's Kitty?" he asked, referring to the scullion. Jason had taken a special interest in Kitty Darrow since her father, Frank Darrow, had been murdered last December, his naked corpse displayed on the wheel of the family's dilapidated mill. It had been a traumatic time for the Darrow family, and Kitty still bore the scars of the tragedy, although she did seem more cheerful these days, perhaps because she'd heard from her brothers, who were rumored to have gone to America.

"It's her afternoon off. Have you forgotten?" Mrs. Dodson asked, looking up from her work.

"Of course. I hardly know what day it is," Jason said with a sigh.

"You look done in, if you don't mind me saying so," Mrs. Dodson pointed out.

"I am. It's been a long day. Would you mind making me a cup of coffee and a sandwich, Mrs. D? I'm starving."

"That's what happens when you miss luncheon," she chided him good-naturedly. She reminded Jason of his mother, whom he missed desperately.

Mrs. Dodson wiped her hands on her apron and set about making the coffee, which she always made in a silver pot fitted with a muslin ring used to filter out the coffee grinds. She set some water to boil, then cut two pieces of bread, added butter, and layered them with thinly cut slices of cold pork. She placed the sandwich on a plate and pushed it toward Jason before fetching a serviette and some milk and sugar for his coffee.

"What's on your mind, Captain?" she asked as she waited for the water to boil.

"I've just paid condolence calls to both the Talbots and the Chadwicks."

"And?"

"And I can't make any sense of this case. Is there any word on Moll?" Jason asked as he took a bite of his sandwich.

"No. The men went out again today, but it's like she fell off the face of the earth. Davy is distraught."

"I just don't understand it," Jason said between bites. "If the killer didn't bother to hide Imogen Chadwick's body, why go to the trouble of making Moll so hard to find?"

Mrs. Dodson looked up at him, her fair hair frothing from beneath her cap like the fuzz of a dandelion.

"What makes you think Moll is dead?" she asked. She spooned some coffee into the muslin and then poured boiling water over it.

"She must be. She's been missing since Tuesday, the same day Imogen Chadwick was murdered."

The wonderful smell of freshly brewed coffee filled the cavernous kitchen, and Mrs. Dodson poured Jason a cup and set it before him. Jason stirred in milk and sugar, but his gaze was on Mrs. Dodson, who seemed deep in thought.

"Davy Brody loves that girl, I'll give him that," Mrs. Dodson said, returning to the croquettes. "But he works her to the bone. Has done since he took her in. She was barely tall enough to reach the counter when he had her serving patrons at the Red Stag. Have you considered that maybe she's had enough?"

"Surely she would have said something, or left a note at the very least. She took nothing with her, not even a change of linen," Jason protested.

"Perhaps she had a pack ready for when she needed it and had hidden it someplace safe."

"And she took off the same day Imogen Chadwick was brutally murdered?" Jason asked. He felt marginally more alert now that the coffee was doing its job.

"Just a coincidence, if you ask me."

"That's some coincidence," Jason replied.

"Imogen Chadwick and Moll Brody had nothing to do with each other. Nothing at all. Why kill them both?" Mrs. Dodson asked. "Makes no sense."

"You are right. It makes no sense whatsoever, which is why it's driving me mad."

"What does Inspector Haze have to say? He must have a theory."

"He's puzzled as well."

"Well, I'm sure between the two of you, you'll solve this murder. You are the eggs to his flour."

"What?" Jason asked, confused by the analogy.

"Just a little baking humor," Mrs. Dodson replied with a smile. "Daniel Haze is a bright man, but his thoughts are loose like flour. Then you come along and add cohesion."

Jason stared at Mrs. Dodson. It was a strange comparison, but it made an odd sort of sense. He and Daniel did work well together and had a way of combining their theories to form—for lack of a better description—a cake.

"So, what does that make you?" Jason asked, grinning at her.

"Sugar. I provide the sweetness," she said, and presented him with a jam tart.

Chapter 21

After his conversation with James Reed, Daniel headed straight into Brentwood. This was proving to be a long day, but he didn't have any time to lose, more so because Moll had yet to be found. After studying the crime scene photographs Ned Hollingsworth had left for him and finding no new clues in the gruesome images, Daniel went in search of Detective Inspector Peterson, who'd had dealings with Lance Carmichael in the past. He tracked DI Peterson down at the Three Bells, where he'd gone for a pint before heading home to his wife and brood of children.

"Afternoon, Haze," DI Peterson called out, raising a hand in greeting. He was a short, wiry man with curling dark hair and gray eyes. The constables at the Brentwood Police Station referred to him as The Hound because he always managed to sniff out the truth.

"Pint?" Peterson asked as Daniel slid into the seat opposite him.

"No, thank you. Still on the clock," Daniel replied.

"You got yourself a corker of a case," DI Peterson said, shaking his head in disbelief. "I've seen the photos. Nasty."

"Yes. And there's another young woman missing."

"Presumed dead?" DI Peterson asked, and took a long pull of his ale.

"I hope not," Daniel replied, realizing that hope was all he had to go on where Moll was concerned. "Where do I find Tristan Carmichael?"

DI Peterson looked at Daniel in surprise. "What's he got to do with this?"

"I have some questions to put to him," Daniel replied. He had no desire to lay out his case, or lack of one, before DI Peterson. He was an experienced copper who might offer sound advice if asked for help, but he was also a cocky devil who might try to take over the case if he had nothing pressing at the moment and managed to convince the commissioner that the case would benefit from the expertise of a senior officer.

"You think he was involved?" DI Peterson persisted.

"He was seen walking with the missing woman on the afternoon of the murder," Daniel admitted with some reluctance. "Does he have a reputation for abusing women?"

DI Peterson considered the question. "I've never heard of him personally laying his hands on any birds, but if the situation called for it, like if one of their whores stepped out of line and no one was around to administer a warning, I have no doubt he'd see to it and do a thorough job. He does like to play at being a gentleman," DI Peterson said. "Doesn't like to be thought of as a thug, our Tristan."

"Is that so?" Daniel asked, wondering how much DI Peterson knew for a fact and how much he was surmising.

"I wouldn't recommend speaking to him in front of his father," DI Peterson continued. "For one thing, he won't tell you anything. For another, you'll make a lifelong enemy of Lance Carmichael, not a prospect that's good for your health or the well-being of those you love."

Daniel felt tension coil in the pit of his stomach. How could he endanger Sarah and their unborn child by putting himself in the path of someone like Lance Carmichael? But, being an inspector, how could he not interview a potential suspect?

"You'll never get him, you know," Detective Inspector Peterson said. "Even if you have the evidence, no judge will convict Tristan Carmichael. Like I said, crossing his father is not advisable, and Tristan being Lance's only son, he'll do whatever it takes to keep his boy safe."

"Thank you, Detective Inspector. I will heed your warning. But I'd still like to speak to the man."

DI Peterson nodded. "Tristan Carmichael oversees several of his father's more colorful establishments here in Brentwood and also in Chelmsford. He arrives unexpectedly, so as to take the managers by surprise and see what they're really up to. He does keep rooms above an opium den. Perhaps you should try there first, but I doubt you'll find him at home so early in the day."

"There's an opium den in Brentwood?" Daniel asked, shocked. He associated the opium trade with places like London and Liverpool, port cities where opium from China found its way into areas most policemen were too scared to go, disappearing into dingy dens frequented by people whose habit ruled their lives and destroyed their families. He wouldn't have thought a rural town like Brentwood was a draw for the dealers, but it seemed he'd been wrong.

"Yes, there is. Probably more than one by now," DI Peterson replied. "The place you're looking for is on Gresham Road. There's a red lantern outside the door."

"What does he look like, Tristan Carmichael?" Daniel asked.

"Have you ever met his father?"

"I saw him in London once, during my days as a peeler. An inspector I was assisting on a case pointed him out to me."

"Tristan looks like a younger version of his father. Tall, fair, and blue-eyed. Face of an angel, some might say. He's well dressed and carries an ebony walking stick with a handle in the shape of a pistol."

"Charming," Daniel muttered.

"Mind how you go," DI Peterson said. "We've no manpower to spare, so you're on your own with this one."

"I understand," Daniel said. What he understood was that like everyone else, the Brentwood police didn't dare cross Carmichael senior. It wasn't worth the risk, not when the constabulary couldn't possibly stand up to an organization the size of Lance Carmichael's.

"Good luck."

"Thank you," Daniel said, and left DI Peterson to his pint.

Stepping outside, Daniel pulled out his pocket watch and checked the time. It had just gone five. It didn't make sense to wait around, so he decided to return home and spend some time with Sarah before coming back to Brentwood later in the evening. He didn't relish the prospect and wished he didn't have to go it alone, but he was an inspector, not a frightened schoolboy, and he'd speak to Tristan Carmichael one way or another.

Daniel found Sarah in the garden. She was sitting on her favorite bench, her hand resting on her belly, a faraway look in her eyes. She smiled when she saw Daniel and shifted to make room for him on the bench.

"I'm glad you're home," she said, and reached for his hand.

"I have to return to Brentwood after dinner."

Sarah instantly looked concerned. "Is it safe to be on the roads after nightfall?"

"I'll be all right," Daniel assured her. "I just have to speak to someone. It won't take long."

"I worry about you, Danny," Sarah said, smiling wistfully. "Why couldn't you have aspired to become a vicar or a schoolteacher?"

"Because I would have been bored out of my mind and would have made for a very dull companion for you."

"You could never be dull," Sarah replied.

"Are you saying you'd be happy with someone like the good Reverend Talbot for a husband?"

Sarah shuddered. "Lord, no. That man's selfishness and indifference to those around him are mind-boggling. I'm so glad Katherine is to be married soon. Jason will be a good husband to her, and he won't allow her father to bully her once they're wed."

"No, he won't. Now let's talk about you. How are you feeling?" Daniel asked.

"A bit uncomfortable," Sarah confessed. "I'd forgotten how difficult the last few weeks of pregnancy can be. To be honest, I can't wait to be alone in my body. And to meet this little one," she said softly.

Daniel laid his hand on her belly. It really was enormous. He felt movement deep inside, the child stirring like some sea creature that had been disturbed in its lair. Daniel felt a pang of fear. So many women died during childbirth, and so many children. Sarah seemed calm and resigned to what was to come, but he was terrified, afraid of losing either her or the child.

"It will be all right, Danny," Sarah said gently, as though she'd read his mind. "We will be all right. I know it."

"If anything were to happen to you…"

"Nothing will happen. Jason will see to that. I trust him with my life," Sarah assured him.

Daniel nodded. Jason had promised to be on hand for the birth of their child, should there be any complications that couldn't possibly be foreseen by Dr. Parsons, whom Sarah couldn't abide. Jason had saved Alice Caulfield and her baby last year, performing a cesarean section on the kitchen table in the dead of night. Alice's little lad, at almost nine months, was healthy and strong, and Daniel found Sarah always searching for him at the Sunday service, her gaze drawn to the little boy as if he were a talisman of some sort.

"Oh, I wish this case were over," Sarah said, dragging Daniel's mind away from the baby. "I don't like it, Danny. I don't like it at all."

"How do you mean?" Daniel asked. No one liked murder, especially when the victim was someone they'd all known, but he could tell there was something else on Sarah's mind.

"There's bad feeling in the village. Tilda said so."

"And how would Tilda know?" Daniel asked, deeply irritated. Tilda had no business frightening Sarah. He'd have a word with her before leaving for Brentwood and tell her to mind herself when speaking to her mistress.

"Don't be hard on her, Danny. I asked her. I like to know what's going on in the village, and I haven't been out in several weeks now. I feel a bit cut off, I suppose."

"Why is there bad feeling?" Daniel asked, even though he already knew. It was always good to hear someone else's take on the situation, even that of Tilda, who was as clever as she was irksome.

"Because the villagers don't care for the Travelers at the best of times, but now there's been a murder, and Moll is still missing. There's talk of retaliation."

"Who's saying these things? Did Tilda tell you that?"

"She didn't name any names, but I would think Davy Brody would be leading the charge," Sarah replied. "Moll is his niece, after all."

"I'll speak to him," Daniel promised. "Tomorrow. Tonight, I'm going to see Moll's beau."

Sarah turned to look him full in the face. "You think he had something to do with her disappearance? Or the death of Imogen Chadwick?"

"I really couldn't say. As far as I can tell, Tristan Carmichael and Imogen Chadwick had nothing to do with each other, and according to Katherine Talbot, Moll seemed happy in his company when Katherine came upon them. What would attract a woman to someone like Tristan Carmichael?" Daniel asked, not really expecting an answer, but Sarah surprised him with her reply.

"Perhaps Moll enjoys a bit of danger."

"You mean she likes to be scared?" Daniel asked, wondering what on earth Sarah meant.

"I mean she might find violence thrilling, as long as it doesn't impact her own life," Sarah explained. "Some women are drawn to volatile men. They think it makes them more masculine, I suppose. And Moll grew up around rough men. I mean, we all know what Davy got up to, and probably still does. To Moll, this might all seem normal."

"Normal?" Daniel echoed. "You think a decent woman can be attracted to a man who's capable of murder?"

Sarah laughed softly. "Katherine is attracted to Jason," she pointed out.

"Are you seriously comparing Tristan Carmichael to Jason Redmond?" Daniel asked, horrified by Sarah's observation.

"Danny, I like and respect Jason Redmond, but he was a soldier during one of the bloodiest conflicts of the century. He's killed. Many times. He had to. The fact that the killing was sponsored by the government doesn't make it any less sinful. Killing as a soldier in war and killing as a soldier in a criminal organization are just two sides of the same coin."

"No," Daniel cried. "A hundred times no. Jason Redmond is an honorable man. Tristan Carmichael is a thug who'll kill anyone who stands in his way. That's not the same as fighting for a cause."

"It is to him. He fights for his own cause versus a cause set out for him by the government. But I think we got off topic, Danny. What I'm saying is that a woman can very easily be attracted to a man of blood as long as she thinks his cause is just, and Moll clearly excuses what Tristan Carmichael does because she believes him to be justified."

"I'm surprised by your reasoning, Sarah, but I do see your point," Daniel said. He felt a pang of guilt because, had the same sentiment been expressed by a man, he'd have found it considerably less shocking and probably would have readily agreed with it. Daniel had never really thought about it before, but he wondered if Jason mourned the men he'd killed in battle and whether his desire to involve himself in investigations was a form of atonement for the sins he'd committed in the name of his country.

And Sarah was right on another point. Daniel admired Jason and thought him a braver man for having been a soldier, especially when Jason had never set out to be one. Daniel couldn't imagine the courage it took to go into battle knowing that you might be killed or maimed. To wake up every morning knowing this might be the last day you'll ever see had to be terrifying, and the fact that a man could return to normal life and still be decent and caring after the atrocities he'd been forced to commit surely made him worthy of respect.

Dragging his mind away from Jason's past, he considered another aspect of the case, wondering what Sarah's take on it might be. She certainly saw things from a different perspective, and surprising as that sometimes was, her point of view was also enlightening.

"Sarah, what would make a woman a threat to someone, in your opinion?" Daniel asked.

Sarah thought about that for a moment. "Well, if the woman turned the head of someone else's man, or perhaps if she possessed a secret."

"I find it hard to believe that Imogen Chadwick could lure someone's man away," Daniel said, wondering if he was being unkind.

"But Moll could. And I wouldn't put it past her," Sarah replied.

"I can't see this murder being committed by a wronged woman. The garrote requires height and strength, and a strong stomach."

"How do you mean?" Sarah asked, clearly horrified by the image Daniel had planted in her mind.

"I mean that it's easier to kill remotely. If you slip someone poison, you don't have to watch them die. You can be elsewhere at the time, ensuring you have an alibi for the time of the murder."

Sarah shivered despite the warmth of the May evening. "How horrible it must be to watch someone die violently. You're right, I can't see a woman choosing the garrote as a weapon, unless that was the only thing to hand. Danny, have you considered that perhaps Moll was the intended victim and Imogen Chadwick simply got in the way?"

Daniel stared at Sarah. He had never once considered that possibility. He assumed Imogen had been the intended victim all along.

"But no one would mistake Imogen for Moll," he said, testing the theory. "Moll is dark and buxom, and Imogen was fair and slight."

"I wasn't suggesting that the killer made a mistake. Only that perhaps they'd wanted to kill Moll, and had done, but Imogen Talbot happened to be in the wrong place at the wrong time and suffered the consequences."

"Oh, Sarah, that's a brilliant theory," Daniel said, humbled by his wife's astute suggestion. "That would certainly put Tristan Carmichael in the frame."

"You shouldn't speak to him alone, Danny. He's a dangerous man. Even I know that."

"I have no choice, Sarah. I must do my job."

"Well, can't you take Constable Pullman with you, for protection?"

Daniel shook his head. "I think a man like Tristan Carmichael will sooner talk to a plain-clothed detective than someone in uniform. Men like him have an aversion to rozzers."

"You mean he might be more forthcoming because his father wouldn't get wind of the conversation?"

"That's what I'm hoping for."

Sarah scoffed. "Surely he won't be so easily duped into revealing something he doesn't wish known."

"No, I don't suppose he will," Daniel replied. "Shall we go in? You look tired."

"Yes. Perhaps I'll lie down for half an hour before dinner. I suddenly feel faint."

Daniel gave Sarah his arm and escorted her into the house, wishing he'd kept his mouth shut and spoken of the weather or Sarah's beloved garden. What kind of fool spoke to his pregnant wife of motive and murder? He really was too caught up in this case to think rationally.

"It's all right, Danny," Sarah said, looking up at him as he helped her up the stairs. "I'm glad you feel you can talk to me about your work. I'm simply tired. It's natural at this stage. It wasn't anything you said."

I doubt that, Daniel thought bitterly, but let the matter drop. He'd be more careful in the future.

Chapter 22

Daniel was back in Brentwood by nine o'clock. Leaving the dogcart at a nearby livery, he walked up Gresham Road, searching for the red lantern. It was a narrow street lined with two-story red-brick houses inhabited by families of merchants and clerks. This wasn't by any means a slum, like London's Seven Dials or Whitechapel. This was a respectable neighborhood. Did the people who lived on this street know that there was an opium den in their midst? Did they mind? Or were they too intimidated to do anything about it, fearing for the well-being of their families and opting to turn a blind eye as long as they deemed themselves safe from the goings-on inside?

The house with the lantern was at the end of the street. Thick drapes covered the windows on the ground floor, not even a chink of light escaping through the folds, but two of the upstairs windows were lit, the curtains parted just enough to reveal something of the high-ceilinged room. Daniel used the brass knocker to announce his presence and hoped he wouldn't be instantly turned away if he asked to speak to Tristan Carmichael. A burly young man opened the door but used his body to block Daniel's view of what lay beyond.

"What do ye want?" he demanded rudely.

"I need to speak to Mr. Carmichael," Daniel said.

"And who might ye be?"

"Friend of a friend," Daniel replied. "It's rather urgent that I speak to him."

"I know all of Mr. Carmichael's friends," the man scoffed. "And he don't know ye."

"I know Moll Brody, and I'm here to speak to Mr. Carmichael regarding her disappearance," Daniel tried again.

The man squinted at Daniel, his indecision obvious. "Ye with the police?" he finally asked.

"Not tonight," Daniel replied, hoping to confuse the man enough to gain admittance.

"Fine. I'll see if 'e wants to see ye. Wait 'ere," he said, and turned away, ready to shut the door in Daniel's face. "Wait, what's yer name?" the man asked.

"Daniel Haze."

The door closed, and Daniel was left waiting on the step. At least he'd found Tristan Carmichael at home, which was fortuitous. If he wasn't allowed in, Daniel would find a place to kip for a few hours and then keep vigil outside the house until Carmichael came out in the morning.

Daniel didn't have long to wait. "Come on in," the man said, stepping aside to allow Daniel to enter. "He'll speak to ye."

The sickly-sweet scent of opium enveloped him in its suffocating grip as soon as he stepped into the entrance hall. The man jutted his chin toward the staircase that hugged the wall on the left, but before Daniel turned away, he peered into the parlor, and the sight made him sick with disgust. He'd never seen an opium den, and although he had a fairly good imagination, he couldn't have summoned up anything like the scene before him. At least a dozen men lay haphazardly around the room, some on velvet couches, others on soiled pallets strewn across the floor. A few still held on to their pipes, but the others had let go of the implements, their eyes closed and their mouths slack, their faces expressionless in their stupor. Judging by the state of their clothes, their unkept hair, and their unshaven chins, many of them must have been there for days, forgoing food, fresh air, and even the most basic hygiene in favor of the sweet promise of the pipe.

"Move along," the man said, giving Daniel a belligerent stare.

Daniel climbed the stairs, eager to get away from the horrible sight. What sort of man would want to come home to this every night? Perhaps Tristan Carmichael no longer saw the prone bodies or the deathlike faces, focusing only on the profit each customer brought. After all, he didn't force these men to come here. He simply provided a service, much like a publican who served men until they were insensible with drink, not caring that some of them drank their wages and left their families to go hungry. Was the publican to blame? Was the purveyor of opium to be held responsible for a man's habit? Daniel didn't have the answer to that, but he certainly didn't feel well disposed toward the man on the other side of the brown-painted door at the top of the stairs.

Daniel knocked and waited nervously, taking an involuntary step back when he heard someone approaching. The door was opened by a middle-aged servant who looked as if he'd seen it all and nothing had the power to shock him. His colorless eyes studied Daniel for a moment, taking in the tweed suit, bowler hat, and round spectacles. If Daniel knew one thing, it was that he looked stolidly respectable.

"You don't have an appointment," the servant said imperiously.

Under other circumstances Daniel would have found that amusing. Did many people make an appointment to see a purveyor of drugs at a time when no respectable person would call on someone?

"No, I don't, but it's important that I speak to Mr. Carmichael. It's about Moll Brody. I told the other man."

"Let him in, Freddie," a voice called from inside the apartment. "I already told you I'd speak to him."

Carmichael sounded irritated, so the servant stepped aside. "Seems you're in luck," he said under his breath. "He never sees anyone at his private lodgings. Come this way."

Daniel was led into a comfortable parlor furnished with a deep-blue velvet sofa and chairs and matching drapes. A thick carpet covered most of the floor, the muted colors a perfect complement to the room's décor. A rather good painting of a pastoral scene hung on the wall behind the settee. A crystal decanter and several glasses occupied a walnut sideboard that matched the elegant end tables, and there was a bowl of fruit overflowing with grapes and oranges that had to have come from some hothouse or tropical locale.

"Well, sit down," Tristan Carmichael invited as he took Daniel's measure. He occupied one of the chairs, his legs crossed, his arms loosely draped over the armrests, his demeanor that of a relaxed man content to spend the evening at home.

"Mr. Carmichael, I'm Inspector Haze of the Brentwood Constabulary," Daniel began as he took the other chair, but Tristan waved the introduction away.

"I know who you are."

That statement took Daniel by surprise, but he didn't ask how Tristan Carmichael knew of him. Instead, he studied his host. With his fair hair falling in gentle waves, his sharp cheekbones and wide blue eyes, he looked like he'd just walked out of a Renaissance painting. All he needed was a whimsical costume and a mandolin to complete the ensemble. His melancholy expression served to reinforce Daniel's impression of him.

"This is about Moll?" he asked, his voice cracking with emotion.

"Yes."

"I hoped it'd be you," Tristan said.

"Did you?"

"Moll likes you. She trusts you. She said you were a good policeman and a kind man."

Daniel was stunned that his name had come up at all, much less in such glowing terms, but did his utmost not to show his surprise, particularly since the man had spoken of Moll in the present tense.

"I was told you and Moll were courting," he began.

"I don't know that I would call it that," Tristan replied. "We are *friends*." His accent on the word *friends* probably implied that there was more to their friendship than mere conversation.

"Does Moll know that?" Daniel asked.

"She does. I've always been honest with her. I could never court Moll openly," Tristan went on. "My father wouldn't allow it. I take it you know who my father is," he added, peering at Daniel.

"I do."

"Well, then you understand. Moll isn't the sort of girl he'd approve of."

"Why not?" Daniel asked, even though he could guess.

"Moll has nothing to offer, at least not to someone like my father. She has no money, no pedigree, and no expectations of inheriting anything of value. My father has other plans for me."

"And you will wed where he tells you?" Daniel asked.

Tristan shrugged. "My father is a very controlling man, Inspector, and I don't care to cross swords with him. I have tried in the past and failed miserably."

"So, you will do as you're told?"

Tristan looked nonplussed. "Inspector, you and I both know that a man doesn't have to love his wife or even spend time with her. I am free to choose my own mistresses, and I have the means to make our liaisons worth their while. I have learned that a man has to pick his battles."

Daniel wasn't the least bit surprised by the answer. He'd heard something similar from Harry Chadwick only that morning. They were nearing the twentieth century, but courtship and marriage rituals hadn't changed much throughout the centuries. Men still married for advantage, and women still sold their virtue to the highest bidder, a transaction sanctioned and strongly encouraged by their parents. Few people married for love, and he momentarily reflected on how lucky he was not to have been born into a family that sought to advance their position through marriage. Neither Daniel nor Sarah had brought money or position to the marriage, but they were happy and free to choose their own destiny.

"And is Moll a candidate for the position of mistress?" Daniel asked, feeling surprisingly sympathetic toward this young man whose whole life was already mapped out for him by a father who'd brook no argument and tolerate no disobedience.

"No."

"Why not?"

"Because Moll isn't looking to be kept," Tristan replied.

"What is she looking for, then?"

"Love, a home of her own, stability," Tristan said. "Beneath the flirtatious façade is a traditional girl who wants marriage and babies."

"You saw Moll the day she went missing," Daniel said.

"Yes. I left my curricle at the Red Stag, and Moll and I went for a walk."

"Matty Locke never mentioned seeing you when questioned," Daniel pointed out.

"He wouldn't have. He's not as stupid as he looks. He knows when to keep his gob shut."

"Meaning that his employer is still smuggling?" Daniel asked.

Tristan gave him a wary look. "Davy's business transactions have nothing to do with this case, Inspector," he said. "Do they?"

"No, they don't," Daniel agreed.

"My visit was of a purely social nature," Tristan Carmichael said.

"How long did you and Moll walk?"

"Over an hour," Tristan said. "We met Miss Talbot along the way. Moll introduced us."

Daniel nodded. That corroborated what Katherine had told Jason. "And then?"

"And then I returned to Brentwood."

"What time did you leave?"

"Around four," Tristan said with a shrug.

"Did you escort Moll back to the Red Stag?" Daniel inquired.

"No. She said she'd come back in her own time. She wished to visit the Gypsy camp," Tristan said.

"Did she tell you why?"

"She wanted to say hello, since they'd only just arrived a day or two before. She seemed eager to see them."

"You were probably the last person to see Moll before she disappeared," Daniel pointed out.

"Yes, I suppose that's true."

"Did you stop anywhere before returning to Brentwood?"

"No. I retrieved my carriage and drove straight back," Tristan said. Daniel was surprised to note that he didn't seem defensive in the least at being questioned thus. He genuinely wanted to help.

"What did you do for the rest of the evening?"

"I saw to some business, then had dinner with a group of friends. I will be happy to furnish you with their names and addresses. I had no reason to hurt Moll, Inspector," Tristan said, his expression earnest.

"Might your father have disapproved of the relationship and taken matters into his own hands?" Daniel asked.

"Inspector, if my father garroted every woman I show an interest in, the countryside would be littered with corpses. Moll and I saw each other only a few times, and before you ask, nothing much happened. I kissed her. She kissed me back. It never went beyond that. I'm not as much of a cad as you seem to think."

"Will you see her again if she's found alive?" Daniel asked.

"Of course, if only to make sure she's well."

"I will take that list of names and addresses now," Daniel said, and waited patiently while Tristan fetched paper and ink and made nine entries. "Thank you for your assistance."

"I truly hope you find her," Tristan Carmichael said, but Daniel wasn't quite finished with him yet.

"Mr. Carmichael, did you know Imogen Chadwick?" Daniel asked as he folded the paper and tucked it into his pocket.

"No, we never met. I am sorry for what happened to her. I read about it in the paper. She didn't deserve that."

"Does anyone deserve to be brutally murdered?" Daniel asked, watching the young man.

"More people than you might imagine," Tristan replied, taking Daniel by surprise.

"Meaning?"

"Meaning that some people are truly evil, and the world would be a better place without them," Tristan explained.

"Do you have anyone in particular in mind?" Daniel asked, wondering if this was a general observation or Tristan had given this some serious thought.

"I do, actually, but I think I'd prefer to keep that information to myself. I assure you, Inspector, that I have no plans to cause anyone grievous bodily harm. What I do for my father is at times distasteful and dishonorable, but I am not a murderer. Unlike my father, I still have a soul, or at least I like to think so, and I will do everything in my power to guard that soul against further corruption."

"Yet you come home to an opium den every night," Daniel pointed out, unable to resist arguing.

"Every man has free will, Inspector, and the men who are currently passed out downstairs have exercised theirs. I'm not responsible for their well-being. If they choose to spend their money on a ball of oblivion, that's their prerogative. Just as it is my right to make a living and earn a profit. Same goes for whoremongers and gamblers."

"You and your ilk take advantage of fallen women," Daniel said, trying hard to hide his disgust.

"I don't compel women to sell their bodies, but I give them a place to do so safely and offer protection against punters who turn violent."

"And you charge them for the privilege," Daniel argued.

"Yes, but they are free to sell their wares in doorways and back alleys. It's their choice. I'm simply a middleman, just like any other businessman who purchases goods and then sells them on. What I never do is try to trick decent women or innocent girls into unwittingly giving up their virtue and then exploit their disgrace. The women we take on are all there of their free will. That is one of my conditions."

"Do you and your father not see eye to eye on that point?" Daniel asked.

"My father and I don't see eye to eye on many points, but I'm sure the same could be said for most young men and their fathers. I will forge my own path, and I will do it on my own terms. Now, if there's nothing else, I will wish you a good night, Inspector."

"Goodnight, Mr. Carmichael," Daniel said, and stood to leave. He felt a grudging admiration for this odd young man who preached moral virtue and the power of free will in a den of sin. Daniel was almost curious to meet Carmichael senior and see what the man had to say for himself. Mostly, Daniel was curious about his feelings toward his son, who seemed on the verge of rebellion.

Freddie showed Daniel out, and he sighed with relief once he was out in the street, breathing in the fragrant night air of late spring. He would check Tristan Carmichael's alibi, but he didn't think Tristan had done anything to hurt Moll. Daniel's gut instinct told him to look elsewhere.

Chapter 23

Friday, May 10

Jason was woken by loud banging. At first, he thought one of the shutters had come loose, but the sound was coming from downstairs and growing louder. He sat bolt upright, now wide awake. Banging on the door usually signified a medical emergency and happened in the middle of the night, since there was no need to rouse the household during the day.

Jason looked toward the window. The sky outside was gray, with thick clouds rolling in from the east, but it was definitely morning. He reached for the pocket watch on the nightstand and flipped it open. Just gone seven. Pulling on his shirt and trousers, Jason hurried downstairs, his bare feet slapping against the polished wooden steps. Dodson, still in his shirtsleeves, hurried toward the door, which was still locked from the night before.

As he yanked open the door, Jason saw a flash of color and the glint of gold, but the person's face was blocked by Dodson's shoulders.

"Please, I must speak to Lord Redmond," a female voice cried.

"Lord Redmond is not receiving—" Dodson began to say, clearly displeased to see whoever it was on the doorstep, but Jason called out to him.

"Let her in, Dodson."

Reluctantly, Dodson stepped aside, revealing the panic-stricken face of Zamfira Lee. Her relief at being allowed to see Jason was palpable.

"Lord Redmond," she cried. "Our camp was attacked last night. People are hurt, and the village doctor won't come. Please, you're a medical man. Help us!"

Jason crossed the foyer in three strides. "Are you hurt?" he asked, casting his gaze over the distraught woman. Her hair was tangled and damp, she smelled of woodsmoke, and her bare feet were covered in mud, but she seemed otherwise unhurt.

Zamfira shook her head.

"Have you eaten?" Jason asked. The woman looked exhausted, and there was a tremor in the hand she lifted self-consciously to her matted hair.

"No." The word sounded like a sigh.

"Dodson, ask Mrs. Dodson to wrap up some bread and cheese for our guest. And a bottle of milk. I need a minute to finish dressing and collect my medical supplies. And have Joe bring the curricle round," Jason instructed.

"Yes, my lord," Dodson replied, his unhappiness impossible to miss. Dodson thought it was bad enough that the lord of the manor was willing to treat the villagers for free, but to allow in a barefoot, filthy Gypsy was unorthodox even for someone as unconventional as Jason Redmond, and Dodson's stony look said he wanted no part of it. Jason might have stopped to explain his reasons, but now wasn't the time, and when all was said and done, he didn't owe the butler an explanation. Dodson was free to find a new position if he couldn't handle Jason's utilitarian views. He turned his back on Dodson and sprinted up the stairs, passing a startled Fanny on his way up.

Jason dressed in record time, then added more supplies to his medical bag, glad that he had purchased the items he'd been running low on the last time he was in Brentwood. Snapping the bag shut, he made his way downstairs.

Zamfira still stood in the middle of the foyer. She held a cloth bundle of food in her hands, her gaze unfocused as she stared around her but likely saw very little. She appeared to be in shock.

"Tell me what happened," Jason invited once she was seated next to him in the curricle and they were driving down the tree-lined avenue toward the gates. "Zamfira," Jason prompted when the woman failed to respond.

"We were worried something like this might happen," she began, her voice low and husky. "Everyone in the village believes we're responsible for that woman's death," she said miserably. "We had no reason to kill her," she cried, and Jason saw the shimmer of tears in her eyes. He reached out and laid a hand on hers, but she pulled it away, spooked by the gesture.

"I'm sorry," Jason said. "Please go on."

"We could have left. We should have left," she said, her voice growing louder, "but leaving would have been an admission of guilt, and we hadn't done anything wrong. We've camped in Bloody Mead every year for generations. We have as much right to be there as anyone."

"I'm not questioning your right to camp in the meadow," Jason said softly. "Tell me what occurred."

Zamfira sucked in a shuddering breath. "Last night, we retired early. Most nights, we sit by the fire, talk, play music and sing, but no one was in the mood. It felt wrong to carry on as normal when that woman had been killed in Luca's caravan only the day before. Everyone retreated to their vardos as soon as it began to grow dark. Normally, Borzo will alert us to strangers in the camp, but he was quiet. We didn't wake until we smelled smoke, and by that time, it was too late. Half the vardos were on fire."

"Did Borzo not bark?" Jason asked, wondering if the fires had been set by someone the dog knew well.

"Borzo was already dead. Poisoned."

"Was anyone hurt in the fires?" Jason asked.

"No, but when we ran outside in a panic, there were people with wooden clubs. They beat us and called us names. They were vicious."

"How many men were there?"

"It was hard to tell. It was dark, and they wore black clothes, hats, and black kerchiefs to cover their faces. There was a woman among them," Zamfira added.

"A woman?" Jason cast his mind over the villagers, trying to imagine which of the country matrons would join the men in an attack against the Travelers, but not a single name sprang to mind. They all seemed like peaceable folk, but people did strange things, even criminal things, when roused to anger.

"Did you recognize anyone?" Jason asked. "Was the publican of the Red Stag among them?"

Zamfira shook her head. "No, I didn't recognize anyone, and they weren't farmers, Lord Redmond. These people were gentry."

"How do you know that?" Jason asked, surprised by Zamfira's revelation.

"Because I know a posh accent when I hear one," she replied bitterly. "It comes through, even when you're calling someone a whoreson, or scum of the earth. It's there, ingrained so deep it can't be so easily disguised."

"And the woman? Did she speak?"

"No, but I heard her laugh. She was enjoying herself."

"What happened after they left?" Jason asked. Hours must have elapsed between the attack and Zamfira's arrival on his doorstep.

"First, we put out the fires. Thankfully, it had begun to rain, but not hard enough to do the job. We had to run to the river and come back with buckets of water again and again. Only a few of us were up to making several trips. Some people were injured, and they grew worse during the night." Zamfira looked like she was about to cry. "And the horses…"

"What about the horses?"

"They slit their throats," Zamfira whispered. "All the horses are dead."

"Dear God," Jason exclaimed. More than most, he knew what people were capable of, but this shocked and disgusted even him. To kill an innocent dog and horses and then to attack people who were sleeping was no different from shooting someone in the back or executing a man who was trying to surrender. Even if these people were guilty of murder, which he strongly doubted, this attack was brutal and calculated, working to ensure that the Gypsies wouldn't return to Birch Hill. And he had a fairly good idea of who would benefit from that.

Jason exhaled loudly when the camp came into view, bracing himself for what he was about to encounter. Smoke hung in the air, blue-gray tendrils rising into the sky from the single cooking fire in the middle of the clearing. Bogdan's wife was bent over a large pot, stirring the contents. The rest of the tribe was seated close to the fire, their eerie silence unnatural given the number of people present. Jason dragged his gaze away from the horses that lay where they had fallen, their shaggy manes spread over the colorful blooms dotting the meadow. He forcibly suppressed memories he had no wish to recall and fixed his gaze on the caravans instead.

They had survived total destruction, possibly due to the rain and lack of wind last night, but there were charred patches where the fires had taken hold, and some of the wheels looked to have been deliberately broken. The caravans would require extensive repairs before they were travel-worthy again, and the Travelers would need new horses if they hoped to leave this place.

Jason spotted Luca Lee, sitting by himself at the edge of the meadow. A furry shape lay at his feet, and Jason didn't need to ask what he was looking at. Luca was mourning Borzo, his head hung low as he cried over his dog. Jason couldn't be sure, but he suspected that the perpetrators had mixed arsenic into whatever food they had used to lure Borzo away from the camp. He only hoped they had used enough to make the death a quick one; otherwise, the poor pup would have suffered unbearably.

Jason jumped out of the curricle and tied the horses to a tree before helping Zamfira out and striding toward the bedraggled group.

"I'm here to help," he said, loudly enough to be heard by everyone. "You have nothing to fear from me. I would like to use one of the less damaged caravans to treat your people," Jason said to Bogdan, who silently pointed toward his own red vardo. "Please come in one at a time, the most severe cases first," Jason said as he stepped into the wagon and set his bag on a chair, taking out the supplies he thought he'd need.

And so it began. They came one after the other, filing in in near silence. Jason treated burns, broken limbs, head injuries, and cuts. There wasn't much he could do for concussions or smoke inhalation, but he gave instructions on how to minimize the damage over the next few days, instructing his patients to rest, drink plenty of fluids, and leave the windows open if sleeping in the charred caravans to avoid compounding the problem. He knew they were frightened and wanted only to hide from further attacks, but they nodded in understanding and stepped aside, allowing the next patient their turn with the doctor.

Jason was tired, hungry, and covered in bodily fluids and soot by the time he'd seen to the last person, a boy of about five who'd been hit with a club on the shoulder and sported a livid purple bruise. Thankfully, the blow hadn't broken his collarbone, or he would have been in great pain and required months to heal properly.

"Please," Bogdan's wife said, beckoning Jason to sit down by her fire once he had come out and washed his hands and face. She handed Jason a cup of ale and a bowl of something that smelled spicy and appetizing accompanied by a hunk of day-old bread.

"Thank you," Jason said. He gulped down the ale, then tucked into the food. It was some sort of stew, but the spices were unfamiliar to him, the flavors foreign. It was good, though, and he finished it all but refused a second helping, thanking the woman profusely.

"It is we who must thank you," she said. "You're a kind man, Lord Redmond. A fair man."

"I have sworn an oath to help anyone in need of medical assistance," Jason replied. "I have a duty."

"Not everyone takes their duty as seriously as you do. The village doctor refused to come. Had his maidservant slam the door in Zamfira's face."

Jason nodded in understanding. What was there to say, after all? He wasn't surprised Dr. Parsons had refused to treat the Gypsies. He was a prissy little man, high-handed and filled with prejudice and disdain for anyone he considered beneath him.

"Please, send for me if there are any complications," Jason said as he stood to leave. "Anytime."

"Thank you," Bogdan said. He held out a handful of coins, but Jason wouldn't take them.

"You don't need to pay me."

"We do," Bogdan insisted. "Please accept the money."

Jason had no wish to insult the man, so he accepted the coins and slipped them into his pocket. He would donate them to an orphanage or some benevolent society claiming to help fallen women. He couldn't keep the payment. It felt like blood money, especially when the Romani now had no mode of transportation with their horses all dead.

Jason returned home to find Daniel waiting for him. The inspector looked at him in astonishment as he walked in, his mouth opening in shock.

"What happened?" Daniel demanded.

"Haven't you heard? The Romani camp was attacked last night. The intruders tried to burn them out, then beat them with clubs. They've also poisoned their dog and killed their horses."

"Dear God!" Daniel exclaimed. "Why did no one come to get me?"

"And what would you have done?" Jason replied bitterly. He could see the answer in Daniel's eyes. He felt as helpless and outraged as Jason did.

"Do you mind waiting while I wash and change out of these soiled clothes?" Jason asked.

"Of course not. Are you all right, Jason?"

"I've seen worse," Jason replied, and trudged upstairs.

Chapter 24

"And how was your day?" Jason asked once he and Daniel were settled in the drawing room, glasses of whisky in hand. Jason had washed his hands and face thoroughly and changed his clothes, but the acrid smell of smoke still clung to his skin and even to his hair, and he looked forward to a hot bath before retiring for the night.

"Not as difficult as yours," Daniel said. "I called on Tristan Carmichael's friends to verify his alibi for the night of the murder."

"And?"

"And they all confirmed it. Of course, it's entirely possible that they'd been forewarned and lied to protect their friend. And it's also just as likely that he was there. The dinner was set for seven, and as far as we know, Imogen Chadwick was already dead by then and Moll was missing, so he could have attended regardless."

"Do you think he did it?" Jason asked.

Daniel shook his head. "I honestly don't. We're missing something, Jason, some vital clue to this case. This wasn't a crime of passion, nor was it a warning from Lance Carmichael to his son. Carmichael senior wouldn't bother to hide Imogen's body in a Gypsy caravan, assuming she was somehow connected to Tristan and posed a threat, nor would he hide Moll's remains. He'd leave her where everyone could see. That's the whole point of a warning."

"Zamfira said the men who attacked the camp had upper-class accents. And there was a woman with them."

Daniel's eyes widened in surprise. "Upper-class accents? Is she sure?"

"She seemed very certain."

Taking a sip of his whisky, Daniel seemed to consider this new information. "Bloody Mead borders land that belongs to the

Chadwicks. They've wanted the Romani dealt with for years, but now that they believe the Gypsies killed Imogen, they think they have license to commit violence."

"My thoughts exactly," Jason said. "Do you think the raid on the camp was organized by Harry Chadwick?"

"Harry Chadwick is not courageous enough to challenge anyone face to face, but under the guise of anonymity, he can be very dangerous—more so because he feels that he has something to prove, not only to his mother, who still treats him like a child, but also to the likes of Sir Lawrence, who's older and saw military action during his days in the army."

Having met Harry on several occasions and known his grandfather, Jason did not doubt Daniel's analysis. Harry was just the sort of young man who'd attack someone under cover of darkness, when his victim was at a disadvantage. "Zamfira said there was a group of them. Do you think Squire Talbot might have been involved?"

"He's the magistrate," Daniel replied, scandalized by the suggestion.

"Imogen was his daughter," Jason pointed out.

"Still, I can't imagine he'd involve himself in such goings-on. I do think Sir Lawrence was there, as well as several men from the Chadwick estate. They might not have wished to participate, but if their livelihoods were on the line, they'd have chosen the lesser of two evils," Daniel suggested.

Jason nodded. "I think you might be right. And the woman?"

"Lucinda," both men said in unison.

"What will you do?" Jason asked.

"What can I do? I have no proof, and there are those, including the magistrate, who'd say the Gypsies got what they deserved and should be grateful the reckoning didn't result in loss of human life. The attack on the camp has also served to prevent them from leaving before the inquest into Imogen's murder, since they will need new horses and time to make repairs to their caravans."

"So, the perpetrators get off scot-free?"

"So it would seem," Daniel replied wearily. "Jason, what are we not seeing here?"

"Let's review what we know so far," Jason suggested. "Imogen Chadwick was unhappy in her marriage and possibly still nursing romantic feelings for James Reed. She sneaked out to go to the Gypsy encampment to have her fortune told, perhaps because she needed to hear that there would eventually be some happiness in her life or to be reassured that she would survive the birth of her child. She made it to Bloody Mead without incident, as far as we know. Having had her palm read by Zamfira, she left, presumably to return home, but for some reason decided to enter Luca Lee's caravan."

"It stands to reason that she either saw something or someone had beckoned for her to enter," Daniel said. "Someone she knew, I should think."

"So, she enters the caravan, and whoever is inside strangles her, either with something they brought with them or something they found in the caravan, such as a violin string. The killer leaves her body where it falls, steps over it to avoid leaving any footprints in Imogen's blood, and gets away undetected."

"Around the same time Moll disappears," Daniel said.

"Tristan Carmichael said that Moll was heading to the Gypsy camp. Might she have seen something and paid for it with her life?" Jason asked.

"I think that's very likely," Daniel replied. "But we still don't have a motive for the first murder. Why was Imogen killed?"

"And by whom?" Jason asked. "Harry Chadwick seems to be the only person who might have wished her dead, but he'd agreed to the marriage, and Imogen was carrying his child. What reason would he have to murder her?"

"Perhaps he'd met someone else he wished to marry," Daniel proposed. "Had he divorced Imogen, there would be scandal, and her father might demand that the assets Imogen brought to the marriage be returned."

"I can't see Harry Chadwick garroting his pregnant wife and then disposing of Moll to cover up the crime. I can't prove he didn't do it, but my gut instinct tells me Harry is not our man."

"What are your reasons?" Daniel asked.

"For one, I don't think Harry has what it takes to murder someone in cold blood and in such a violent manner. For another, Moll is not only taller and stouter than Imogen, but she's also stronger. She's used to physical work and can carry several full tankards of ale in each hand, a feat that requires great dexterity and strength. Had Harry gone for her, Moll would have put up a hell of a fight and would have screamed loud enough to attract attention. As it stands, the search party has found no signs of struggle, and no one claims to have seen or heard anything. If Moll is dead, then she was killed quickly and efficiently by someone who either took her by surprise or has killed before and knew precisely how to silence her before she had a chance to fight for her life."

"And who, in your opinion, fits that description?" Daniel asked.

"Daniel, is there any reason, no matter how far-fetched, why the Romani would want to kill Imogen Chadwick?"

"Not that I can conceive of. What would they have to gain by her death?"

"Nothing but trouble," Jason replied. "Which they have already been on the receiving end of."

"I hate to say it, but I think this case might go unsolved. The facts as we know them don't add up to a theory," Daniel said, sighing heavily.

"Perhaps we need to rearrange the facts," Jason said, his expression thoughtful.

"How do you mean?" Daniel asked.

"All this time, we've been assuming that Imogen was killed first and that her murder had been planned. We've treated Moll's disappearance as secondary, leaving Davy to organize search parties and hunt for clues while we focus on Imogen Chadwick's death. We recognize that the two events are probably connected, but we don't know how, and we're assuming that whatever happened to Moll was a byproduct of the murder. But what if Moll was the intended victim all along, and Imogen's murder was secondary?" Jason suggested.

"Who would want to kill Moll Brody, and why? We haven't come across anything that ties Moll into Imogen's murder, nor do we know for certain that Moll is dead. But there's another possibility we haven't looked at," Daniel said excitedly, amazed he hadn't considered this possibility sooner. "What if Imogen Chadwick was murdered by Moll?"

"You mean Moll arrived at the Gypsy camp after leaving Tristan Carmichael, found Imogen Chadwick on her own, lured her into the caravan, killed her, and fled?" Jason asked, astounded by how well the facts fit this new theory. "But why would she kill Imogen Chadwick? What would be her motive?"

"Perhaps Imogen had done something to hurt or humiliate her. She might have found out about Moll's Romani father and taunted her with it," Daniel suggested. "I doubt Davy Brody is the only person in Birch Hill who knows the truth. Squire Talbot, for all his outward indifference, is aware of everything that goes on and might have known about Moll's parentage all along. Perhaps he'd let something slip, or Imogen had overheard him mention it to someone else. Young people can be cruel, and she might have thought it amusing to bait Moll. Perhaps she'd threatened to reveal the truth. Moll's life would never be the same if people knew."

"Which might have incensed Moll enough to want to silence her, except for one minor detail," Jason mused. "By all accounts, Imogen Chadwick was a shy, reticent young woman. Colorless, Micah called her. Can you see her taunting a barmaid?"

"Under normal circumstances, no," Daniel replied. "But if Moll had done something to hurt Imogen first, such as perhaps flirt with Harry in front of Imogen or allow her to believe that Harry had been intimate with her, Imogen might have retaliated by resorting to using the one thing sure to hurt Moll the most. Everyone has their breaking point, Jason, and even though Imogen didn't seem to love her husband, that doesn't mean she wouldn't have been devastated to learn that he was being unfaithful to her, and so soon after the wedding. And as you have just pointed out, Moll is taller, broader, and has strong hands that could easily pull on a garrote hard enough to almost slice Imogen's head off."

"Yes, in theory, that makes sense," Jason agreed. "But we don't have any tangible proof that this is the way it happened," he pointed out. "It's all supposition."

"But this new theory does fit the facts." Daniel looked at Jason pointedly. "Jason, you said you can't imagine Harry Chadwick committing such a violent murder. Can you see Moll Brody perpetrating such an act?"

Jason thought about that for a moment. "My heart says no, Moll is not capable of such violence, but my head says Moll is just passionate enough to act on her feelings. If she did kill Imogen Chadwick, it wouldn't have been a premeditated act."

"Yes, I believe you might be right. Perhaps some sort of altercation took place between the two women, and Moll seized her chance." Daniel set down his glass and stood, feeling like a man twice his age. "I think it's time I went home. I'm glad we were able to cobble together a plausible theory, but I have to admit, it is with a heavy heart that I leave you."

"I like Moll as well," Jason replied. "I hope to God we're wrong about this."

"So do I," Daniel said. "I would not wish to see Moll hang."

Chapter 25

After Daniel left, Jason called for hot water and retired to his bedroom. He was looking forward to a long soak. As he watched Henley haul up buckets of hot water, Jason decided that once he and Katherine returned from their wedding trip, he would begin modernizing the manor and install proper plumbing throughout the house. It was high time the place had running water. It would be costly but worth every farthing. He wanted Katie to have the best of everything, and having to wait nearly an hour for enough hot water to fill the tub really was ridiculous. Mrs. Dodson would benefit as well. How much easier her daily work would be if she could simply turn on a tap and fill her pots with water or wash her hands whenever she wanted to. And Kitty would be able to wash vegetables and scrub pots without having to constantly fetch water from the outside, a task she didn't relish, since the buckets were too heavy for a girl of her slight build to carry.

Once the tub was full, Jason got in and was finally able to wash off the scent of smoke and the tang of blood that had clung to his hands since leaving the Gypsy encampment. Once finished, he lay in the bath until the water had grown lukewarm, enjoying the peaceful sensation of being submerged. He was reluctant to get out, but once the bathwater had grown uncomfortably cold, Jason toweled off, donned his dressing gown, and settled in the armchair by the window. He planned to read until it was time to dress for dinner, but was interrupted by Micah, who knocked on the door and entered without waiting for Jason to reply.

"Are you all right?" Jason asked once Micah seated himself on the side of the bed.

"I think Mary wants to leave," Micah said in a small voice. "She wants to return to America."

"Yes, she told me." He watched Micah as he waited for him to continue. Would this be the moment Micah told him he'd be leaving as well?

"I don't want to go," Micah said. "I like it here."

"You are welcome to stay," Jason replied. "You know I don't want you to go."

"But what about Mary? She's my only blood family."

"Micah, I will look after Mary and make sure she and Liam are safe and well, and you can see them again soon."

"I can visit?"

"Of course. In fact, maybe Katherine and I will visit as well. I do miss New York, and I'd like to show her all my favorite places."

"It's not fair, though," Micah said with a dramatic pout. "Why does she have to leave when we've only just found each other again?"

"Because she wants to marry, and if she marries someone here, she'll have to stay forever," Jason explained.

"Why can't she just marry Mr. Sullivan?" Micah said wistfully. "She likes him; I know she does. He's a good man, and he'd be a loving father to Liam."

"Micah, a marriage between Mary and Mr. Sullivan is impossible. His affections are engaged elsewhere."

"I really don't understand romance," Micah said, his face like a thundercloud. "What makes someone fall in love?"

"Well, there are shared interests, common goals, and also physical attraction."

Micah looked blank. "How do you mean?"

"I mean that when you love someone, you want to touch them, and kiss them, and eventually make love with them."

"Kissing is gross," Micah said. "Why would anyone want to suck on someone's mouth?"

Jason laughed. "It's hard to explain, but you will understand once you meet someone you find attractive."

Micah thought about that for a moment. "I think Arabella Chadwick is pretty," he said, his face becoming dreamy. "It didn't look gross when that man kissed her."

Jason sat up straighter. "What man?"

"I don't know his name, but Tom said he works for the squire. Keeps his books and such."

"You saw him kiss Arabella Chadwick? Where?"

"At the boathouse. Tom and I hid behind the trees and watched them for a while." Micah giggled.

Jason frowned, suddenly recalling that he'd meant to ask Micah about his visit to the Gypsy camp. "Micah, what time did you go to Bloody Mead on Tuesday?"

Micah blanched. "You know about that?"

Jason nodded. "Surely you know by now that you can't hide anything from me."

"I should, shouldn't I?" Micah grumbled. "It was after my lessons with Mr. Sullivan. Around half past three, I suppose."

"Did you go alone?"

"No, I went with Tom, and we didn't really go to the camp. We just skulked around," he said sheepishly.

"Did you see Imogen Chadwick?" Jason asked.

Micah nodded. "Yes, we saw her walking through the woods. At first, I thought it was Arabella Chadwick. They look alike, don't you think? But then I saw the hair. Arabella's hair is like spun gold," Micah said dreamily. "But Imogen Chadwick's hair is very fair, like her mother's."

"Was Imogen alone when you saw her?" Jason asked, hoping to focus Micah's attention on the details rather than Arabella Chadwick's charms.

"She was at first, but then Arabella caught up to her and they argued."

"What about?" Jason asked, his breath catching.

"I don't know. Tom and I were too far away to hear, but it looked heated. I did hear Imogen say, 'I'll tell everyone if you don't stop.'"

"And then?"

"And then Tom and I left. Tom had to go help his father, and I was getting hungry and wanted to be back in time for tea."

"Why didn't you tell me this before?" Jason demanded, a knot forming in the pit of his stomach as he considered the implications of what Micah had just shared.

Micah hung his head. "Because Mr. Sullivan had given me extra reading to do, and I said I would read in the garden, on account of it being such a nice day, but then I sneaked out because I'd promised Tom to meet him. I didn't want to give myself away. How did you know, anyway?" he asked miserably. "Did Mr. Sullivan come to check on me?"

"The Travelers saw you and Tom and mentioned it to me when questioned."

Micah nodded. "I'm sorry."

"For what? For lying to Mr. Sullivan or not telling me sooner?"

"Both, I suppose. Am I to be punished?" he asked, looking at Jason with trepidation.

"I will not punish you for going to the Gypsy camp. You were curious; I can understand that. But you lied to Mr. Sullivan, and that I cannot ignore. You are to spend the rest of the evening reading in your room."

"What about dinner?"

"You can have a light meal in your room."

Micah slid off the bed. "I'm sorry. I know I did wrong, but you don't have to starve me."

"I wouldn't call a tray in your room starvation." *And I know Mrs. Dodson will send up something tasty the moment I turn my back*, Jason thought. "Now, off with you."

Once Micah left, Jason considered the situation. What the boy had seen shone a whole new light on the murder because now Jason could see a clear motive. If Imogen had discovered that Arabella had been seeing James Reed, a man she'd obviously loved, she'd had something over Arabella, who would suffer greatly if her secret came out. Not only had Arabella been jilted by her fiancé, but now her purity might come into question. Few young women could recover from that type of vicious gossip and still make a good marriage. Arabella's prospects would be radically diminished if potential suitors believed she'd had a premarital affair.

But would Arabella really kill her oldest friend, and in such a gruesome manner? Was she capable of such an act? It was hard to say. And what did Arabella hope for when it came to her relationship with James Reed? Surely she didn't expect to marry him. Caroline Chadwick had ambitions for her daughter and would never permit Arabella to squander herself on a glorified clerk. Arabella would have to end the affair sooner or later. Wouldn't she?

And how did Moll figure into this? Jason got off the chair and began to pace. It helped him to think. It would be a lot easier to formulate a plausible theory if he knew what had become of Moll. Was she the killer or a second victim? And if she was, had she been the intended victim all along or simply collateral damage? He'd have to speak to Daniel about what he'd learned tomorrow, but one thing was clear—Arabella Chadwick was hiding something.

Jason glanced at his watch. Henley would be there in a few minutes to help him dress for dinner. One would think he had a dinner engagement, the way formalities were observed for simple, everyday tasks. What was wrong with going down to dinner in one's shirtsleeves? After all, he was dining with Mary and Shawn Sullivan, not the bloody queen and her entourage.

A knock on the door interrupted Jason's little internal tantrum. *Like clockwork*, Jason thought, and called for Henley to enter. He was surprised to see Dodson hovering in the doorway.

"You're wanted, sir."

"Is it the Romani?" Jason asked, hoping there hadn't been another reprisal against the hard-hit Travelers.

"It's Mrs. Haze, sir."

"Is Inspector Haze downstairs?" Jason asked.

"No, sir. He sent a message, asking you to come as soon as you can."

"I'll be right down," Jason said as he began to dress hurriedly. He grabbed his medical bag, made sure it contained a scalpel, laudanum, and plenty of clean gauze, and rushed downstairs and into the purple twilight.

Chapter 26

Jason jumped out of the curricle, tossed the reins to the boy who'd come out to greet him, and strode toward the house. The door was opened by Tilda, who took his coat and hat and directed him upstairs. Jason met Daniel halfway up the stairs. Daniel's face was tight, fear in his eyes.

"Is something wrong?" Jason asked, trying to figure out if this was the natural nervousness of an expectant father or barely controlled panic caused by a complication.

"I don't know," Daniel muttered. "Sarah says she's all right, but I don't think she is. It was Harriet who asked me to send for you."

"Pour yourself a drink and try to keep calm."

"Are you politely asking me to keep out of the way?" Daniel asked, his mouth twitching as he tried to smile and failed.

"That is exactly what I'm asking you."

"You'll let me know if anything is wrong?"

"Of course. Now go."

Sarah was in her dressing gown, walking the length of the corridor with the support of her mother. She smiled wanly at Jason, but he could see the lines of pain etched into her pale face. She was panting and her forehead glistened with sweat.

"Sarah, how are you?" Jason asked as he took in her demeanor. "How far apart are the contractions?"

"Five minutes," Harriet Elderman replied. "I've been timing them."

"So, we have a bit of time," Jason said.

"I think there's something wrong," Harriet said softly.

"What makes you think that?" Jason asked, hoping this was just normal anxiety.

Harriet looked furtive for a moment, as if she wished they could speak in private, but then, after stealing a peek at Sarah, she said, "I don't think the child is in the right position for birth."

Jason nodded in acknowledgement. "Sarah, will you permit me to examine you?"

"Yes." Sarah's voice was weak and trembling. She was in a lot more pain than she was letting on, probably for her mother's and Daniel's sakes. Sarah made her way toward the bedroom, where a stack of fresh towels and a baby blanket had been prepared for the birth.

"Mrs. Elderman, if we might have a moment," Jason said when he realized that Harriet intended to be present for the examination. He followed Sarah into the bedroom and shut the door.

"Would you have felt more comfortable with your mother here?" Jason asked, realizing he should have consulted Sarah before asking Harriet to wait outside.

"No," Sarah said. She grimaced as a contraction seized her, her face turning red as she unwittingly held her breath.

"Breathe," Jason said. "Just breathe through it."

"Easy for you to say," Sarah grunted.

"Focus on me," Jason said. "Let's breathe together." He sat down on the side of the bed and reached for her hands, forcing her to meet his gaze. Jason took a deep breath and exhaled. Then did it again. Sarah followed suit. Once the contraction passed, Jason seized his chance. "Do you feel that something is wrong?" he asked. A woman always knew, especially one who'd had a child before.

Sarah nodded, her eyes filling with tears. "Yes," she whispered. "Something is wrong. I know it."

"Lie back for me."

Sarah slid down and stretched out her legs, pressing them together. Jason placed both hands on her belly and moved them around slowly, searching for identifiable body parts. It didn't take long to outline the position of the baby.

"I must perform an internal exam," Jason said.

Despite the pain, Sarah was visibly mortified at the thought of him probing her in such an intimate way, but he had no choice. He needed to know precisely what they were dealing with.

"All right," Sarah muttered. She raised her legs and planted her feet on the bed, parting her knees a few inches. Jason quickly washed his hands in the basin and approached the bed.

"Sarah, you needn't be embarrassed," Jason said as he gently pushed her legs further apart and slid his fingers inside her, working his hand in until he felt the child inside.

"Jason, what is it?" Sarah asked as he continued to probe, his other hand now on her belly. "Jason?" she cried when he didn't respond. "What's happening?"

Jason yanked out his hand just as another contraction rolled in and waited for it to pass before speaking to Sarah, who wouldn't have been able to focus on anything but the pain.

"Sarah, what we're dealing with is a transverse lie. That's when the baby is positioned horizontally instead of vertically with the head down, which is the optimal position for delivery."

"What does that mean?" Sarah asked, her voice quivering with fear.

"It means that the child will lead with the shoulder, which will make delivery more difficult."

"What are you not saying?" Sarah persisted. "Is the child likely to die? Am I?"

"The situation is not ideal, but that doesn't mean either of you will die. You are not fully dilated yet. There's still time to turn the child around."

"You can do that?" Sarah asked, her eyes pleading with him to reassure her that he could help.

"I can't guarantee it will work, but I would like to try, with your permission."

"And if it doesn't work?" Sarah asked. She licked her dry lips and took a shuddering breath.

"If it doesn't work, then I will put you to sleep and perform a cesarean section. I've done it before," he said in his most reassuring manner.

"I know. The Caulfield baby."

"Yes."

"Do what you must," Sarah said. "Try to turn it."

"It will be painful," Jason warned. "Shall I call your mother in?"

Sarah shook her head. "I want Danny," she whispered. "I need Danny."

"Of course."

Jason opened the door and came face to face with Harriet, who looked pale and frightened. "Mrs. Elderman, you are right, the child is not in the right position. I will try to turn it in utero, but if I'm unsuccessful, a cesarean section will be required."

Harriet's hand flew to her mouth. "No!" she moaned. "I can't lose my girl. Please, if it comes down to a choice between Sarah and the baby, save Sarah."

"I will do everything in my power to save both mother and child. Now, please ask Daniel to come upstairs. Sarah wants him with her."

"No husband should have to see that," Harriet sputtered.

"Mrs. Elderman, time is of the essence," Jason reminded her. "This is what Sarah wants."

"Of course. I'm sorry. I will send Daniel up right away." She hurried toward the stairs, leaving Jason alone in the corridor.

He wasn't a praying man, hadn't been since he'd seen the slaughter that had been the Civil War, but he took a moment to pray for the safety of Sarah and her baby. This wasn't a random stranger as Alice Caulfield had been when he'd sliced her open on the kitchen table. This was Sarah Haze, and he'd never forgive himself if his poor judgement resulted in her death, or that of the baby.

Jason faced Daniel across the expanse of the corridor.

"Jason," Daniel choked out. "What do I do?"

"You remain calm and support Sarah no matter what. If she sees your fear, she will be even more frightened than she already is. I will do everything I can, Daniel. And I might need your help."

"To do what?"

"To turn the child. Are you ready?"

"Yes," Daniel answered without a moment's hesitation.

Sarah's face looked sickly in the glow of the gas lamp, her eyes wild with fear. Her lips were moving, probably in prayer.

"Sarah, I need you to lie flat on your back," Jason said. "And try to breathe normally. Don't hold in your breath when I press down on your stomach."

"All right," Sarah said. She sounded terrified.

Once Sarah was in position, Jason turned to Daniel. "Daniel, place your hands on Sarah's belly. Right here," Jason showed him the exact spots. "When I tell you to, I want you to push up with one hand and down with the other, like so." Jason demonstrated without putting any pressure on Sarah's stomach.

"What will that accomplish?" Daniel asked.

"Ideally, this will dislodge the child and push its hips upward while pushing the shoulder downward, directing the head into the birth canal."

"Dear Lord," Daniel muttered under his breath. "What if it doesn't work?"

Jason gave Daniel a warning look. "It will work," he said with more confidence than he felt. He was not an obstetrician. He would feel more confident in performing a cesarean section, but he had to try to avoid major abdominal surgery if there was another way. It brought him comfort to know that his scalpel was clean and ready in his medical bag, the magic wand he could rely on to perform a miracle if it came to it.

Jason waited until the next contraction passed, then looked at both Sarah and Daniel. "Now," he said. "Daniel, wait for my command."

Daniel's eyes widened with shock when Jason slid his arm between Sarah's legs and pushed his hand inside her up to the wrist, making Sarah cry out in pain. He felt around until he could identify the baby's shoulder and hip, then very carefully began to push the hip upward.

"Now, Daniel. Press where I showed you." Daniel pushed his hands down and pressed.

"Harder," Jason instructed.

Sarah was panting hard, her face glistening with sweat. She was trying not to scream, but Jason knew she was in terrible pain. "Again," he said, and pushed from beneath.

Daniel winced at Sarah's sharp intake of breath and pushed again. Sarah moaned pitifully, but Jason ignored her.

"Again," he said as he continued to angle the child's bottom away from the pelvic floor. He felt the infant shift marginally. If he removed his hand now, it might slip right back into the same position.

Jason found himself holding his breath as a contraction seized Sarah, the muscles tightening around Jason's hand and squeezing his wrist until he thought it would break. He took deep breaths but maintained his hand on the child's hip, waiting until the contraction ended to push.

"Now," he said to Daniel once the pressure subsided. He was trembling, his hand numb from the vise-like grip of the contraction. "Press as hard as you possibly can."

"I'm hurting Sarah," Daniel protested.

"I know, but it must be done. Sarah, can you bear it?"

"I'm fine," Sarah panted. "Just do it."

It took another twenty minutes and five contractions, but then, at last, Jason felt the child slide sideways, and his fingers brushed against the curve of the skull. He pulled out his hand and wiped it on a towel before laying his hands on Sarah's belly. He could make out the child's hips, now aligned with Sarah's own, and the hard knob of a knee. He prayed the child wouldn't flip again, so kept his hands on Sarah's belly to prevent the infant within from moving.

"Sarah, recline against the pillows. They will give you extra support. It's time to push," Jason said. "You're very nearly there. Give it all you've got."

Sarah took a deep breath and bore down, a blood-curdling scream erupting from somewhere deep inside her chest.

"Again," Jason said.

Sarah pushed, and pushed. She was sweating and red in the face, her damp hair sticking to her forehead. Daniel appeared to have lost the ability to speak, but he did hold Sarah's hand and mop her brow.

"One more," Jason commanded, exhaling in relief when the baby crowned. "We're nearly there. Push hard."

Tears of pain and frustration ran down Sarah's cheeks, but she bore down again and again until the baby slithered from between her thighs right into Jason's waiting hands. He quickly cut the cord and cleaned the child's airways, his gaze fixed on the infant's bluish face. Jason placed his hand over the tiny chest. He could feel the heart beating, but the child had yet to take a breath. Jason lifted the baby and gave it a hearty slap on the bottom. An outraged howl filled the room, and they all let out the collective breath they'd been holding.

"Oh, thank God," Sarah exclaimed.

Jason wrapped the child in a blanket and held it out to Sarah. "A perfect baby girl," he said. "Congratulations. Daniel, breathe," he added. Daniel looked like he was about to pass out.

Having been reminded, Daniel drew in a deep breath. His eyes shimmered with tears. "Sarah, she's so beautiful."

"She is," Sarah agreed. "Jason, thank you. You saved her."

Jason didn't reply, his vision blurred by tears of relief. He could barely feel his right hand, so performing surgery would have been tricky had it come to that. They had all gotten lucky this night, he decided, as he flexed his fingers to get the circulation going.

"Have you picked out a name?" Jason asked, looking at the happy family.

"Charlotte," Sarah said. She looked besotted with the bundle in her arms. "I'd like to name her Charlotte."

"Whatever you want, my dear," Daniel said softly. "I think Charlotte Haze sounds very nice."

"May I come in now?" Harriet asked as she stuck her head in the door. "I want to see my granddaughter."

"Of course," Sarah replied. "Come in, Mama. Look how sweet she is."

Charlotte yawned hugely and opened her eyes for just a moment, delighting her parents and grandmother.

"I'll leave you to get acquainted," Jason said. "Daniel, I'll need to speak to you first thing tomorrow, if you're able to spare the time."

"I will call on you immediately after breakfast," Daniel promised, his adoring gaze never leaving his daughter's face.

"I'll say goodnight, then." Jason washed his hands, picked up his bag, and made his way downstairs.

"Is there anything I can get you, sir?" Tilda asked.

"No, thank you. Just make sure your mistress eats well and takes plenty of fluids. Send for me if she develops a fever."

"Yes, sir. Goodnight, sir."

"Goodnight."

Jason stepped out into the cool evening, surprised to note that it was close to midnight. Stars twinkled in the velvety sky, and a gibbous moon shone bright, bathing the trees beyond the gate in a silvery glow. Regardless of the outcome of the investigation, he would always remember today as a particularly good day.

Chapter 27

Saturday, May 11

Daniel looked exhausted and bleary-eyed when he arrived at Redmond Hall the following morning, but the blissful expression on his face warmed Jason's heart.

"How is Sarah? And the baby?" Jason inquired as he invited Daniel to join him in the drawing room.

"Both well. I confess, I didn't sleep a wink. I just kept watching them, my mind going over all that could have gone wrong."

"But it didn't. You have a beautiful family. Enjoy it."

"I'm so glad you were there, Jason. I don't think the outcome would have been the same had Dr. Parsons attended on Sarah."

Jason clapped Daniel on the shoulder in the universal gesture of camaraderie. "Would you like some coffee? It might revive you."

Daniel looked like he was about to refuse, then changed his mind. "Please."

Jason rang the bell pull and asked Fanny for a pot of coffee, then turned to Daniel, who was watching him. "I'll stop by in a few days to check on Sarah and Charlotte, if that's all right," Jason said.

"Of course. You don't need to ask my permission." Daniel looked a bit embarrassed as he met Jason's gaze. "I wonder if there's something I might ask you."

"Anything," Jason replied, assuming Daniel might ask about resuming marital relations or something about caring for the baby.

"Jason, I know we haven't known each other long, and you might decide to leave Birch Hill at some point, but do you think you might consider becoming Charlotte's godfather? Sarah and I would be greatly honored if you were to accept."

Jason's face split into a grin. "Of course. I'd love to. It is my honor to be asked."

Daniel breathed out a sigh of relief, as if he had expected Jason to decline. "Thank you. Sarah will be glad to hear the news."

Fanny entered the room carrying a tray. She set it on the low table, poured out coffee for both men, and added milk and one cube of sugar to Jason's, the way he liked it, before asking Daniel if he'd like milk and sugar as well.

"Yes, please," Daniel said, watching Fanny make his coffee as if she were performing some sort of chemical experiment.

"Mrs. Dodson sent up some teacakes," Fanny said. "In case you were peckish."

"Thank you. And tell Mrs. Dodson she always knows just the thing," Jason said as he reached for a cake. "Daniel, try the cakes," he invited. Daniel looked in need of sustenance.

Daniel helped himself to a cake and ate it, then took several sips of coffee. "I'm actually getting used to this stuff," he said. "It's not as vile as I originally thought." He took another sip. "Last night you said you had something you wished to discuss with me," he reminded Jason, looking marginally more alert.

"Daniel, I had an interesting conversation with Micah yesterday. It seems he sneaked out to meet Tom Marin, and the two of them headed to the Gypsy camp on Tuesday afternoon. The boys witnessed an argument between Imogen and Arabella, which Micah described as heated. Imogen threatened Arabella."

"With what?" Daniel asked, sitting forward in his eagerness to hear what Jason had to say.

"Exposure, most likely. Micah often visits Tom, and they roam the Chadwick estate. The boys have seen Arabella and James Reed at the boathouse, kissing."

"So, Imogen discovers Arabella is being romanced by the man of her dreams and demands that Arabella end the relationship, or she'll tell?"

"Something along those lines. That certainly gives Arabella a motive, given what exposure might do to her reputation and prospects for the future."

"Is Arabella physically strong enough to have committed the murder?"

"If Arabella was able to maintain the pressure on the garrote long enough for Imogen to quit struggling, then I think she could manage it."

"And Moll?" Daniel asked, reaching for another cake.

"Moll is several inches taller than Arabella Chadwick. I don't see how Arabella would be able to get the garrote around her neck, unless Moll was seated, her back to Arabella. If she were facing her assailant, she'd see what was about to happen and fight for her life."

"Nor do I see Arabella digging a grave deep enough to bury Moll. There'd be evidence of her efforts."

"Yes," Jason agreed. "Arabella's hands would be blistered, even if she'd worn gloves. Her hands were bare when I paid the condolence call, and I saw nothing to suggest that she'd done any heavy digging in the past few days."

"She might have had an accomplice," Daniel suggested.

"My thoughts exactly. How do you mean to proceed?"

"I'm going to question James Reed again, then speak to Arabella. And I would also like to interview Davy Brody. I have some questions to put to him."

Jason nodded in agreement. "However, I think we need to question Tom Marin first."

"Yes, I agree with you," Daniel said. "Shall we go now?"

"I've asked Micah to invite Tom here. They should be here shortly."

"Good thinking," Daniel said. "If we go barreling onto the Chadwick estate, we'll be showing our hand."

"Exactly. I have no doubt the killer is nearby, watching carefully to see what we will do, and right now they believe themselves to be safe, since we appear to be poking in the dark. Let's not give up our advantage."

"Are you certain you don't want to become a detective?" Daniel asked, smiling at Jason over the rim of his cup.

"I don't think my future wife would approve of that career choice," Jason replied, grinning back. "It's bad enough that I dissect cadavers as a hobby. I should consider myself lucky she doesn't think me ghoulish."

"Ghoulish to some, scientifically minded to others. It's all a matter of perception, and Katherine Talbot is a very perceptive woman."

"That she is," Jason agreed.

"We're here," Micah called out as he burst through the door, Tom Marin shuffling behind him.

"And not a moment too soon," Jason said, nodding approvingly at his charge. "Have a seat, Tom. Teacake?" he asked, all innocence.

Tom Marin looked from the lord of the manor to the police inspector, his gaze growing alarmed. Despite his fear, he perched on the edge of the settee, reached for a cake, and took a dainty bite, chewing slowly as he awaited their pleasure.

Chapter 28

"Micah tells me you've seen Arabella Chadwick and James Reed at the boathouse," Jason remarked conversationally. He leaned back in the armchair and crossed his legs, looking as relaxed as if he were simply chatting to a friend.

Tom looked at Micah, who nodded in encouragement before snatching a teacake off the plate. "Yes, my lord. I've seen them a few times," Tom muttered. "I like walking by the lake."

"And what were they doing when they met?" Jason asked.

"They talked. And kissed," Tom whispered, his embarrassment obvious. "They were all over each other." He made a face of disgust.

"And how often would you say they meet?" Daniel asked.

"I don't know exactly, but Miss Arabella did ask me to deliver a message for her a few times. She gave me a coin for my silence," Tom added, clearly uncomfortable to be betraying Arabella's confidence but eager to please Jason with this important tidbit.

"Did she, now?" Jason asked, nodding in approval. "Did she give you a letter for Mr. Reed or a verbal message?"

"A note, sir. She told me not to show it to anyone or she would get into trouble. And she never told me his name."

"And did you go to Mr. Reed's office to deliver the message?" Daniel asked.

"No. I'd wait for him on the footpath."

"And did he ever give you an answer to pass on to Miss Arabella?" Jason asked.

"A few times he asked me to tell her he'd be there."

"Did he give you a coin as well?" Jason asked, the corner of his mouth lifting in a smile. Tom nodded.

"You're a very enterprising young man," Jason said. "Have you seen anyone else meet at the boathouse?"

"No," Tom said, shaking his head.

"Are there any other places on the estate where someone can meet in secret?" Jason asked.

"There's the 'ermit's 'ut," Tom replied, looking at Jason earnestly.

"Sorry, what?" Jason asked, looking confounded.

Daniel tried to suppress a smile, already anticipating Jason's reaction to the explanation.

"The 'ermit's 'ut," Tom repeated. "That's where the 'ermit used to live, but 'e ran off."

"There was a hermit living on the Chadwick estate?" Jason asked, looking even more confused.

"Of course," Tom said. "You should get one."

"What does one do with a hermit?" Jason asked. He looked at Daniel for an explanation to this odd suggestion.

"Keep 'im to entertain yer guests, my lord. Mrs. Caroline always brought her visitors to visit the 'ermit. They'd ask 'im questions, and such."

"I'll explain later," Daniel chimed in. They were wasting valuable time.

"Right. So, the hermit ran off and the hut's been empty," Jason summarized. "And have you seen anyone use it to meet in secret?"

Tom looked uncomfortable but answered the question. "I've seen my da meet Mrs. Chadwick, 'round Christmas, that were," he whispered. "She were angry with 'im. 'E told me not to tell my ma when I asked 'im about it, but ma already knew. She knows everything."

"And have you seen them meet since?" Jason asked.

"No. Mrs. Chadwick doesn't summon da no more. Ma said the she-wolf 'as tired of 'im at last."

Jason decided not to pursue this line of questioning but filed away the information for later use. If Caroline Chadwick and John Marin had been conducting an affair, it wasn't for him to apprise his son of the fact. There was no reason to suspect that either John Marin or Caroline Chadwick was involved in Imogen's murder, if the affair had ended at Christmas.

"Tom, have you ever seen anyone argue?" Jason asked.

"Like who, my lord?"

"Like Imogen and Arabella Chadwick, for instance," Jason remarked.

"Just that one time, the day of the murder. They really went at it, 'ammer and tongs," Tom said. "Mrs. Imogen were really angry."

"And have you ever seen Moll Brody on the Chadwick estate?" Daniel asked.

Tom thought about that for a moment. "I saw 'er walking with that cove as drives a posh carriage and 'as fine horses," Tom said dreamily. "They wasn't on Chadwick land, though. They was in the lane. That were on Tuesday."

"Did they look friendly?" Jason asked.

"They looked well pleased with themselves, my lord," Tom said, smiling at the memory. "The cove gave Moll something, and she started to cry."

"What did he give her?" Daniel asked eagerly.

"I couldn't see. It were something small. Then she threw 'er arms about 'im and kissed 'im."

"Tom, what do you know of James Reed?" Jason asked, watching the boy intently.

Tom shrugged again. "Not much. 'E likes to walk in the woods and 'e's always friendly when 'e sees me. 'E gave me a boiled sweet once."

"Do you see him often?" Daniel asked.

"'E walks every day, round the same time, as long as the weather is fine."

"What time is that?"

"Round three."

"And when was the first time you saw him with Arabella Chadwick?" Daniel asked.

Tom's brow knitted in concentration as he considered the question. "End of March, I think. After the family returned from London, but before Mr. 'Arry and Mrs. Imogen returned from their wedding trip."

"Have you ever seen Mr. Reed meet with anyone else?" Jason asked.

"Like who?" Tom asked.

"Like Lucinda Chadwick," Jason supplied.

"Nah. Miss Lucinda don't like to walk. She likes to ride. She goes out in the mornings with 'er groom."

"And does she like her groom?" Jason asked, tilting his head innocently.

Tom laughed. "No, she 'ates 'im. She calls 'im a clumsy oaf and always tries to lose 'im. She likes 'er freedom, Miss Lucinda. She don't care to be chaperoned."

"And what does she do when she leaves him behind?" Daniel asked softly.

Tom shrugged. "Nothin'. She just gallops."

"And what about Harry Chadwick, Tom?" Jason asked. "Do you ever see him?"

"'E liked to take the boat out on the lake sometimes," Tom said. "That's why 'e built the boathouse, to keep 'is boat in. But 'e don't use it so much anymore."

"Did he go out in the boat alone?" Daniel asked.

Tom nodded.

"And have you ever seen Mr. Harry meet with anyone in secret?" Jason asked, his disappointment obvious. So far, Tom hadn't told them anything they didn't already know, except that he sometimes acted as a go-between for Arabella and James Reed.

Tom stole a peek at Micah, who'd lost interest in the conversation and was staring out the window with ill-disguised longing. Tom lowered his voice. "I seen 'im with Mr. Sullivan, sir. They met at the 'ut." His voice was almost a whisper.

Micah's head spun round, his gaze fixed on Tom, his mouth open in astonishment. "Harry Chadwick is friendly with Mr. Sullivan?" Tom nodded, his expression one of guilt.

"You never said," Micah chastised Tom.

"I didn't—" Tom began to explain, but Jason cut him off.

"Thank you, Tom. Micah, I think it's time for your lessons." He took a coin out of his pocket and handed it to Tom. "For your trouble, Tom."

"It's no trouble," Tom replied, reluctant to take the coin.

"Think of it as payment for valuable information," Jason said. "You've earned it."

"Thank ye, sir," Tom said, and finally accepted the coin. He stuffed it into his pocket. "Did I really 'elp?"

"You did," Jason assured him. "Micah will see you out."

After the two boys left, Daniel and Jason exchanged looks.

"So," Jason said. "Caroline Chadwick argued with John Marin, and by the sound of it, their relationship had ended last Christmas. It would be remiss of us not to consider the possibility that Imogen Chadwick had blackmailed either or both of them, but given what we know of the woman, I find that highly unlikely."

"I agree," Daniel said. "What would Imogen have to gain by blackmailing either of them except a world of trouble? And if the relationship fizzled out last year, why bring it up now?"

"Could Moll have been the blackmailer?" Jason asked.

"Again, why now?" Daniel mused. "Rumors of a liaison between Caroline Chadwick and John Marin have been circulating for at least a year, and I can't imagine that Caroline would stoop to murder to put them to rest."

"Maybe not, but if Sir Lawrence got wind of those rumors, he might reconsider marrying into the family," Jason argued. "With Sir Lawrence Foxley, Baronet, visiting," Jason mimicked, "this would be the perfect time to blackmail Caroline."

"I seriously doubt Sir Lawrence would be put off by a discreet fling conducted by a middle-aged widowed woman, not when Lucinda's sizeable fortune is at stake. Do you?"

"Probably not," Jason agreed. "Then, we have Harry Chadwick meeting with our very own Mr. Sullivan, and Arabella Chadwick's romance with James Reed."

"Do you suppose Harry Chadwick and Shawn Sullivan…" Daniel allowed the sentence to trail off, his meaning crystal clear.

"That would certainly explain why Harry Chadwick was happy to have separate bedrooms and showed little interest in his wife," Jason said.

"And why he agreed to marry Imogen Talbot in the first place. A more sensual woman might not have been happy with the arrangement, but Imogen didn't want him in her bed any more than he wanted to be there."

"She might have confronted him," Jason pointed out. "Having a homosexual husband is not an easy thing to accept, even if you don't love the man. Do you think Harry might have killed his wife because she threatened to expose him?"

"Why would Imogen risk the scandal? She was carrying his child. Imagine what that would do to that child's future prospects if it were widely known that its father was a molly," Daniel added. "Where was Mr. Sullivan on Tuesday afternoon and evening?"

"He was here. I can vouch for him. After their lessons, Mr. Sullivan was in the library, researching something, then I saw him walking in the garden with Mary. We had a game of chess before dinner, then he went up to change. His movements for the time of

Imogen's murder are fully accounted for. I do think a word with Mr. Sullivan is in order, given what we've just learned."

"I'll leave that to you," Daniel said. "When will you speak to him?"

"There's no time like the present," Jason said, and pushed to his feet. "Will you wait?"

"Oh, yes," Daniel replied, and reached for the last teacake.

"And after I've finished, you can explain to me why someone would keep an ornamental hermit on their land and bring their guests to see him as a form of entertainment. It might take me some time to wrap my uncouth American brain around the concept, but I'll give it my best try," Jason said, rolling his eyes in mock exasperation.

Chapter 29

Jason found Mr. Sullivan and Micah in the middle of a math lesson. Shawn Sullivan had the usual harried look when dealing with Micah's reluctance to apply himself to his sums, but instantly rearranged his features into an expression of calm. His brows lifted in surprise when he spotted Jason outside the partially open door.

"Mr. Sullivan, a word, please," Jason said, earning a look of gratitude from Micah.

"Is everything all right, my lord?" Shawn Sullivan asked as he joined Jason in the corridor.

Jason led him to an empty room that had at one time been occupied by his father's nursemaid and shut the door. Shawn Sullivan looked distinctly uncomfortable but refrained from questioning his employer. Instead, he waited patiently, only his gaze betraying his anxiety at this unexpected interruption.

Jason exhaled deeply, wishing he didn't have to put the poor man on the spot. Everyone had a right to their secrets and sins. What right did he have to strip away the façade of propriety this poor man had erected to protect himself and those dear to him? But it had to be done, and he would tread as carefully as he could, given the delicate subject he was about to meddle in.

"Mr. Sullivan, I'm afraid I must ask you some personal questions. Normally, I would never demand that you account for your private time, but I believe that what you have to impart will help Inspector Haze apprehend a killer, so I beg your pardon in advance. And please know that nothing you share with me will endanger your position here or alter my regard for you," Jason added hastily, seeing the blood drain out of Shawn Sullivan's face, making his ginger hair seem even brighter in the light streaming through the window.

"Of course, my lord," Mr. Sullivan mumbled.

"Are you conducting a love affair with Harry Chadwick?" Jason blurted out.

Jason thought the poor man was going to be sick. His hand went to his belly and he hunched forward, drawing in his shoulders as if to protect himself against a blow. He took several shaky breaths before finally replying.

"Yes. Harry Chadwick and I have met several times over the past few months."

"Is it serious between you?" Jason asked.

"I'm not sure what you mean, sir," Mr. Sullivan replied. He was taking short, shallow breaths, and his face went from deathly pallor to a feverish flush in a matter of moments.

"I mean, do you have feelings for each other, or is this just a..." Jason couldn't bring himself say *sexual liaison*.

"What does it matter, Lord Redmond?" Shawn Sullivan exclaimed. "Even if Harry and I are in love, it's not as if we could ever be together. We snatch a few private moments when we can. That has to be enough."

"Shawn," Jason said gently. "Did Imogen blackmail her husband with his homosexuality?"

Shawn Sullivan looked genuinely surprised. "No. She never knew."

"Are you sure?"

He nodded. "Imogen was glad to be left alone, and once Harry discovered she was with child, he was happy enough to let her be. They had separate bedrooms, and the arrangement suited them both. She even told him she wouldn't mind if he took a mistress as long as he didn't trouble her in that way until they were ready to try for another child."

"Does anyone know Harry prefers men?" Jason asked.

Shawn Sullivan shook his head. "Harry has taken great pains to hide his true nature. He's even gone to a brothel with Sir Lawrence while in London. He didn't have relations with the girl, only had her—" He went quiet, unable to finish the sentence.

"Never mind," Jason said. He could guess what the man was alluding to.

"Imogen's death has come as a blow to Harry, my lord. Now he will face pressure to remarry and sire an heir, and his next wife might not be as sexually timid as Imogen was."

"And what of you, Shawn? Has he made you any promises?" Jason asked gently.

"No, and I don't expect any. I was unable to continue with my former relationship once I came here," Shawn said miserably. "My partner ended things between us months ago. We still see each other as friends from time to time, on my day off, but he's moved on. Harry and I recognized each other's need and agreed to meet in secret to assuage our loneliness. That doesn't mean either of us expects this to become a permanent arrangement. Harry has his responsibilities, and I will leave here once Micah is ready to go away to school, unless you'd like me to leave now," he added, his gaze pleading with Jason not to dismiss him.

"I don't want you to leave, Mr. Sullivan. I'm happy with the work you are doing, and your secret is safe with me. It always will be. Thank you for trusting me with your innermost feelings."

Shawn Sullivan nodded. "Thank you, my lord. May I return to my duties now?"

"Of course."

Returning downstairs, Jason quickly related the gist of the conversation to Daniel, who listened in amazement.

"I never suspected Harry Chadwick of leaning that way," Daniel said. "I almost feel sorry for him."

"So do I," Jason said. "But I do think it's safe to rule him out as a suspect. It would be in his best interests to keep his wife alive and use her as a shield against suspicion. Also, the child would certainly have taken the pressure off, leaving him to pursue his own romantic goals unhindered. And given Imogen's less-than-worldly nature, I don't believe she would ever have suspected her husband of being romantically involved with a man. It simply wouldn't have occurred to her."

"I don't think it's occurred to anyone," Daniel replied.

"It seems that Harry works hard to maintain the illusion of a man about town, even visiting a brothel with his future brother-in-law to preempt suspicion. I don't believe he's our man," Jason said.

"Neither do I," Daniel agreed. "But I do think it's urgent that we speak to James Reed. And I'd like you to come with me."

"With pleasure."

Chapter 30

They opted for Daniel's dogcart instead of Jason's flashier curricle and set off for the Talbot estate. No one challenged them, and the grooms who were working at the stables did nothing but tip their caps and get on with their chores. Daniel wondered if someone might alert Squire Talbot to their presence, but they'd be finished with the interview by then, or so he hoped. He had no desire to involve the squire in the investigation, more so because the man could hardly be impartial when his own daughter was the victim.

James Reed was at his desk, an open ledger before him. "Good morning, gentlemen," he said, looking up in some alarm. "Is something wrong?"

"Not at all, Mr. Reed," Daniel said. "I would just like to speak to you for a few minutes. This is Lord Redmond," he said, introducing Jason but not offering a reason for his presence. "May I?" he asked, pointing to the guest chair.

"Of course. I'm afraid I don't have another chair. Here, take mine, your lordship."

"Please don't get up, Mr. Reed. I'm happy to stand."

James Reed looked from one man to the other, his eyes full of anxiety. "How can I help, Inspector?"

"Mr. Reed, it has come to my attention that you are—for lack of a better word—friendly with Arabella Chadwick."

James's cheeks suffused with color, but he didn't bother to deny the allegation. "Yes, I'm quite fond of Miss Arabella. How did you—" he began, but Daniel cut him off.

"And where do you normally meet, Mr. Reed?"

"When possible, we meet at the boathouse on the Chadwick estate. It's quite remote, so there's little chance of being seen."

"But seen you were," Daniel reminded him. "Mr. Reed, what are your intentions toward Arabella Chadwick?"

"I—I love her," James Reed choked out.

"That doesn't answer my question," Daniel pointed out. "Arabella Chadwick is the daughter of a wealthy, influential family. You are an estate manager. How do you see this relationship progressing?"

James Reed bowed his head, studying his hands, which were clasped on his desk. "I never expected a future with Arabella. It was enough for me just to spend some time with her."

"Mr. Reed, did you know that Imogen Chadwick was aware of your relationship?" Daniel asked, watching the man intently.

James Reed's head shot up, and he looked genuinely surprised. "No. That's not possible. Arabella would have never told Imogen. It would have been too much of a risk."

"Nevertheless, Imogen knew, and it seems she had threatened Arabella with exposure on the very day she died."

Jason studied the man, watching the meaning of Daniel's words take root.

"Are you suggesting...?" James Reed let the question trail off, clearly unable to say the words out loud.

"Arabella had a motive for killing Imogen Chadwick, yes," Daniel replied, his gaze pinning the man to his chair.

"No! Arabella would never hurt anyone, least of all her dearest friend."

"Yet she was carrying on with the man Imogen had been in love with, and probably still was at the time of her death."

"Look, Inspector, I never led Imogen on. I never promised her anything or even realized how deeply her feelings for me ran. I was simply being polite to the daughter of the house. And Imogen was married and expecting her first child at the time of her death. Why shouldn't Arabella and I have spent time together? Neither of us owed Imogen anything other than friendship."

"And yet, Imogen had the power to hurt you both. Arabella's reputation would suffer, and you would most certainly lose your position for sneaking around the Chadwick property when you should have been working."

"I am allowed to take an hour for my lunch," James Reed replied calmly. "I eat at my desk and then take a walk later in the day. Squire Talbot knows this. I didn't do anything wrong."

"Except court Arabella Chadwick in secret, knowing full well that she would suffer if the truth were to come out. Arabella and Imogen were seen arguing, presumably about you, the day Imogen Chadwick was murdered. The altercation took place just before the estimated time of death. What have you to say to that, Mr. Reed?" Daniel demanded.

James Reed sat back in his chair and glared at Daniel, an insolent smirk marring his handsome features. "All you have is supposition, Inspector. There's not a shred of proof that Arabella is responsible for Imogen's death. Nothing that will stand up in court, at any rate. People argue all the time. And then they get on with their lives. Imogen was a kind soul. She never would have done anything to hurt Arabella, certainly not when Arabella was her only ally in that house, so I really think you're barking up the wrong tree, Inspector, as your lot so often seems to do. Imogen was murdered by the Gypsies. You are the only one who seems to doubt that. Now, if you don't have any more questions for me, I must get back to work."

"Good day, Mr. Reed," Daniel said as he pushed to his feet. "I'm sorry to have disturbed you."

The two men stepped into the shadowed yard and walked toward the dogcart, each lost in his own thoughts.

Chapter 31

"Well, that went well," Jason said once they left James Reed's office and climbed into the dogcart.

"He's right, you know. It's all supposition. Arabella had the most obvious motive for the murder, and she had the opportunity. She was seen arguing with the victim shortly before her death and was probably the only person to know that Imogen had sneaked out of the house and wouldn't be missed for hours to come. She was also in the vicinity of Moll at the time of the murder, which suggests that there might have been some sort of an altercation between the two women that resulted in Moll's death."

"I don't think you should rule out James Reed as her accomplice," Jason said. "Had Imogen outed his relationship with Arabella, he'd not only lose his lady love, but likely his livelihood, and find himself cast out into the world with no character reference after working for Squire Talbot for years, which would be catastrophic. He was quick to point out that he'd done nothing wrong, but he was known to take a daily walk in the late afternoon, right around the time of the murder. Arabella could have murdered Imogen, but she's not tall or strong enough to take on Moll. But James Reed is, and he's strong enough to hide the body."

"Did you happen to notice his hands?" Daniel asked.

"I did, yes. His hands appear unmarked, but that in itself is not proof that he wasn't involved."

"Without proof, there's no case. I think there's only one way to bring about a resolution," Daniel said.

"We must flush out the killer," Jason said, completing Daniel's thought.

"Yes, but how?"

Jason pulled a folded sheet of paper out of his pocket and held it up triumphantly.

"What's that?"

"An order form James Reed had filled out. It was pinned to the wall behind his chair. I slipped it into my pocket while he was focused on you."

"And what good will this form do us?" Daniel asked, perplexed.

"The form in itself, not much, but the sample of the handwriting and the signature are another matter entirely. Roger Henley happens to be a very talented young man who has an aptitude for forgery. He doesn't know I know this, but Mrs. Dodson let it slip that he'd forged past employers' signatures onto character references he'd written himself to hide evidence of his drinking. She said the signatures were identical."

"What are you suggesting?" Daniel asked, his eyebrows lifting in surprise.

"I'm suggesting we arrange a meeting between Arabella Chadwick and James Reed, with each informing the other that the relationship is over. James and Arabella are bound to have an argument once they meet, or at the very least hash the situation out to their mutual satisfaction. We will be there to witness the outcome."

Daniel considered the idea. It was certainly worth a try. The worst that could happen was that they'd learn nothing of value, but if the ruse worked, either James Reed or Arabella might allow something vital to slip. "But we don't have a sample of Arabella's handwriting," Daniel said, focusing on the details instead of fretting about the possibility of success.

"Katherine and Arabella corresponded frequently while the Chadwicks were in London. She'll allow me to borrow one of the letters if I ask nicely."

"And who will deliver these notes?" Daniel asked.

"Tom Marin. They've used him to send messages before, so neither will have reason to get suspicious."

"You think this might work?" Daniel asked, still a bit dubious.

"I think we will learn enough to determine whether either of them was involved, and maybe discover what's become of Moll."

"And if we don't?"

"Then we'll go back to the beginning and try to reason this out," Jason said.

"All right," Daniel said. "Can I leave you to arrange this? To be honest, I can hardly focus on the case when all I can think about are Sarah and Charlotte." He smiled wistfully.

"Go home, Daniel. Spend some time with your family. I will send a message as soon as I have everything arranged. Will three o'clock be convenient for a meeting? We mustn't wait too long in case the lovers decide to meet on their own before we have a chance to observe them."

"That seems to be around the time they normally meet, so neither one should suspect a ruse. I will wait to hear from you," Daniel said as he dropped Jason off at Redmond Hall.

"My regards to Sarah." Jason tipped his hat and strode inside.

Chapter 32

Despite his longing to be with Sarah and the baby, Daniel decided to stop off at the Red Stag to speak to Davy Brody. He didn't like the man, and the feeling was mutual, but he had to speak to Davy about Moll. He would be remiss if he didn't interview Davy in person, and perhaps Davy had managed to remember something from the day Moll went missing, something he hadn't shared with Jason.

Daniel left the dogcart with Matty Locke and entered the tavern. The interior was dim and cool, and the usual smell of fermenting hops and baking bread hung in the air. The taproom was still empty, but Daniel was surprised to see Mrs. Etty come out from the kitchen, an apron tied around her narrow waist.

"Good morning, Inspector," Mrs. Etty said, smiling warmly at Daniel. "I 'ear congratulations are in order."

"Yes. Thank you. A girl," Daniel replied. He knew he was beaming.

"May she live a long and healthy life," Mrs. Etty said. Coming from a woman who laid out the village dead, the benediction held extra meaning for Daniel, especially since it had been Estelle Etty who'd laid out Felix after he died.

"What are you doing here, Mrs. Etty?" Daniel asked.

"Davy can't manage the place on 'is own, not without Moll. So 'e asked me if I might step in for a spell, just until things settle down."

Daniel supposed that by *settle down*, Mrs. Etty meant that Moll would turn up, alive or dead.

"That's kind of you, Mrs. Etty. Is Davy around?"

"'E's in 'is office," Mrs. Etty said, gesturing to a door behind the counter. "I'll tell 'im ye're 'ere."

"Go on in," Mrs. Etty said when she returned a few moments later. "Davy's waiting for ye."

Daniel stepped behind the counter and entered the small office. Davy sat behind his desk, a small leather-bound notebook before him. About a dozen crates of spirits were stacked against the walls, and a film of dust covered every surface. Daniel assumed Moll had been the one to clean the room, but with her not there, Davy hadn't bothered.

"What can I do for ye, Daniel?" Davy asked. He looked tired and careworn.

"I'm sorry for what you're going through, Davy," Daniel said sincerely. "I wish I could do more to find Moll."

Davy inclined his head in acknowledgement. "Ye're doing what ye can," he said gruffly.

Daniel took a seat across from Davy. "Have you heard from Lance Carmichael?"

"No. Why would I? Ye think he 'ad something to do with this?" Davy asked warily.

"It's a possibility," Daniel said. He didn't think Lance Carmichael had anything to do with Imogen Chadwick's death, but there was a slim chance that Moll's disappearance had nothing to do with the murder, and Daniel had to pursue it, just to be sure.

"It weren't Lance as done for 'er," Davy said.

"How do you know?"

"Because I know Lance. 'E loves Tristan more than life itself. Tristan is 'is only son, 'is darling boy. Lance might not approve of everything Tristan does, but 'e'd never risk losing 'im. So, if Tristan wants Moll, Lance will bite 'is tongue and wish them well."

"You really believe that?" Daniel asked. This didn't align with the picture of Lance Carmichael Daniel had in his mind.

"Even the 'ardest man 'as a soft spot if ye look 'ard enough."

Daniel nodded. He supposed Moll was Davy's soft spot. Always had been, since he didn't have any children of his own.

"Davy, can you recall anything Moll might have said or done? Was she frightened? Could she have been planning something?"

"Like what? Like a dash to Gretna Green with Tristan? Neh. Moll was her usual cheery self. She weren't frightened, and she weren't planning nothing either. She'd 'ave told me if she were. We're close, Moll and me. Always 'ave been. She tells me everything, she does, like I were 'er own father."

Daniel studied the man across from him. Davy had spoken of Moll in the present tense, which didn't mean anything in itself since it was natural to hold out hope for her return, but there was something in the man's gaze that gave Daniel pause. Davy was certainly tired, having been running the Red Stag almost singlehandedly and searching for Moll all hours of the day. He was understandably wary, given his past troubles with the law, but Daniel didn't get the sense that Davy was grieving. Beneath the worn exterior he was calm, collected.

"Will you be organizing another search party?" Daniel asked.

"No. What'd be the point of that? We've combed the area round Birch Hill. Moll ain't 'ere, at least not above ground," he added.

"Davy, I will do everything I can to discover what happened to her," Daniel promised as he stood to leave.

"I know ye will, Daniel. Look, I'm sorry for our past trouble," Davy said, giving Daniel a look that could only be described as earnest. "Ye were only doing yer job. I get that. It weren't yer fault I were breaking the law."

And still are, Daniel thought.

"I wish ye luck with this case. It's a tricky one, to be sure, but I know ye'll solve it. Ye're smarter than most, and that Lord Redmond, well, 'e's a card, ain't 'e. Never seen the likes of 'im." Davy rose to his feet and held out his hand, which Daniel was forced to take. "Bygones?" Davy asked.

"Bygones," Daniel replied. He wondered if Davy hoped Daniel would turn a blind eye the next time Davy got caught red-handed, but it didn't matter, not today.

Daniel left the tavern and headed home to spend some time with Sarah and his baby girl, his heart soaring with impatience.

Chapter 33

"Do you really believe Arabella killed Imogen?" Katherine asked, staring at Jason in horror, her fingers plucking at the lace trim on her sleeve, something she did when she was upset.

"I believe she was involved," Jason replied, going for the gentler truth. "Inspector Haze and I have been able to rule out nearly every other suspect. Arabella had a motive, she was seen arguing with Imogen just before her death, and she has no alibi for the time of the murder."

"You are asking me to help you trap her," Katherine said miserably.

"Yes, I am. I'm also asking you to trust me."

Katherine's troubled gaze met his. "I do trust you." She got up and walked over to a small desk situated between two windows that overlooked the village green. She opened a drawer, extracting a stack of letters. She flipped through them until she found what she was looking for and handed the letter to Jason.

"Here, I hope this helps."

"It will," Jason said, and pocketed the letter. "Katie—"

"No," Katherine said, holding up her hand to ward off whatever he was about to say. "I don't want to talk about it. Do what you must. And for the love of God, Jason, be careful."

"Thank you," Jason said, and left the vicarage to avoid another run-in with Reverend Talbot. He was in no mood to explain what he was up to.

By the time Jason returned to the hall, Henley had penned a letter to Arabella from James Reed, and Micah had summoned Tom.

Jason held out Arabella's letter to Henley. "Can you do it? Can you forge a woman's handwriting?"

Henley smiled confidently. "I can forge anything, my lord," he said cockily, then instantly backtracked. "Nothing illegal, mind you."

"No, of course not," Jason muttered. "Get on with it, then. We don't have much time."

The boys were in the kitchen, enjoying freshly baked scones with jam and clotted cream, when Jason came downstairs in search of Tom.

"Are you ready to do your bit to solve this murder, Tom?" Jason asked, hoping he wasn't putting the boy in harm's way.

"Yes, sir," Tom said, jumping to his feet and hastily wiping a bit of jam off his chin.

"Off you go, then. I'll be waiting to hear from you."

"Yes, sir," Tom said again. He pocketed both letters and took off, Micah looking after him wistfully.

"I wish I could have gone with him," Micah said.

"That might give our plan away," Jason replied.

"Not really. People see me with Tom all the time."

"Nevertheless, I think it's best if you wait here. Care to give me a game of chess?" Jason asked.

"Sure," Micah grumbled. "I get to move pieces around a board while Tom helps solve a crime."

Jason grinned. "All right. Would you like to help me prepare instead?"

"How?" Micah asked, his eyes narrowing in suspicion.

"Clean my Colt."

"Really? You mean it? Can I practice shooting, just to make sure it's working properly?"

"Sure, why not," Jason said. Micah was an excellent shot and knew his way around a gun. Jason would never trust him with the Colt otherwise. He hadn't planned on taking the pistol this afternoon but decided that at least one of them should be armed, since Daniel never carried a weapon.

By the time Micah had cleaned the gun and had fired off a few shots, Tom came back, breathless and excited.

"They'll both be there, my lord."

"Well done," Jason said, and tossed Tom a coin, which the boy caught deftly with his left hand. "And I don't want either of you anywhere near the boathouse. You hear?" he commanded, looking from one boy to the other. He could almost taste their disappointment.

"We'll keep our distance," Micah whined.

"No. You are to stay here. Do I have your word?" Jason asked, skewering Micah with his gaze.

"You have my word," Micah replied, hanging his head in dejection. "I never get to do anything fun," he muttered under his breath, the Colt already forgotten. "Come on, Tom. Let's go do something respectable and deathly dull."

The boys shuffled off, leaving Jason to wait for Daniel and brood. This was meant to be a happy time. Jason was to be married in a few weeks, and Daniel had a newborn daughter and a wife who needed him. Instead they were hunting a killer who was uncomfortably close to home. Jason could hardly forbid Katherine to visit the old and sick, as she did every week, but he worried about her walking around by herself when two young women had already been victimized.

Detection was based on reason and logic—looking for clues, unearthing motives, and identifying the suspects were the building blocks of solving a case. But sometimes, there was no logic. There were people who simply enjoyed killing. He'd seen it during the war years. Most soldiers carried the men they'd killed in their hearts, asking for their forgiveness and worrying about what would become of their families, but there were those who worried they hadn't killed enough men, soldiers who'd reveled in taking a life and enjoyed watching someone's suffering. Spilling blood was an aphrodisiac to them, and they often needed a woman immediately after the battle, desperate to slake their bloodlust on some grubby camp follower who was only too willing to service their needs.

What if Jason's instincts were wrong and there was such a person in their midst? What if Imogen had been a random victim whose death served to ease someone's need for violence? And what of Moll? Was her body decomposing in some shallow grave, her radiant smile and laughing eyes now frozen features on a death mask no one would ever see? What if Katie or Mary or Kitty was next?

Jason sprang to his feet, angry with himself for giving in to doubt. He had to listen to his gut instinct, which told him he was on the right track. There were those who killed for pleasure, but most people killed for a reason, and those reasons were surprisingly simple. Greed, fear, anger, and sometimes love. And he had a feeling this murder had been committed for all of the above.

Chapter 34

Daniel finally arrived at a quarter past two, and he and Jason set off on foot. Jason thought that would give them enough time to walk to the boathouse and get into position before either Arabella or James Reed arrived at the meeting place. Thanks to Micah and Tom, they had a good description of the boathouse and the surrounding area, which would enable them to keep out of sight while still remaining close enough to observe the meeting between Arabella and James.

The boathouse was a simple affair, a barnlike structure with a peaked roof, wide enough to store one rowboat, with a wooden walkway running along the three walls, each fitted with a small window, and a door on the right side to access the boathouse from dry land. Except for the boat itself, two pairs of oars, and a coil of rope, there was nothing of interest, and no place to hide. The structure smelled of pine and lake silt and backed onto the woods.

Daniel walked around the boathouse, then pushed open the small window in the back wall, ensuring they would hear the conversation should Arabella and James decide to talk inside. With each man positioned to the side of the back window behind the structure, they'd have a passable view of the inside and could see the path leading to the boathouse.

Murky water lapped at the walkway and the empty boat, and the forest was full of birdsong, whispering leaves, and the skittering of small animals. Otherwise, the place was deserted, which would enable Arabella and James to speak freely without fear of being overheard. The only thing that could spoil the plan was if the two decided to walk around the lake, making it impossible for Jason and Daniel to follow for fear of being seen, but walking would also expose the courting pair, which was hardly in their best interests. They were sure to keep close to the boathouse if they hoped to keep their meeting private. Taking up their positions behind the boathouse, Jason and Daniel settled in to wait.

James Reed was the first to arrive at five to three. He entered the boathouse, exited, having ascertained that Arabella wasn't inside, then returned and began to pace along the wooden walkway like a man who was driven by a mechanism he couldn't stop. He wore a suit of brown tweed that did nothing to drab down his good looks, and his bowler hat sat at a rakish angle on his head, the ensemble completed by a handsome walking stick that he gripped with a gloved hand and tapped on the wooden walkway to punctuate his steps.

Arabella made an appearance at three minutes past three, her black gown and bonnet making her look like a ghost that had decided to walk by day, no less spectral in the sunlight. Jason didn't have a clear view of her face since she walked with her head down, but her shoulders were tense, and her hands were balled into fists at her sides. This wasn't a woman anticipating a romantic tryst with the man she loved.

"Bella," James exclaimed as soon as she entered the dim confines of the boathouse. "Please, don't let what happened drive a wedge between us."

He took her by the upper arms and looked down into her face. Arabella looked up, confusion marring her lovely features as she tried to make sense of what James was talking about. Her silence seemed to spur him on.

"The police have nothing concrete against you. It's all supposition. If you keep your silence, they will be forced to direct their inquiries elsewhere."

Arabella's mouth opened slightly, her eyes widening in shock as she took in what James had said. "Inspector Haze thinks I killed Imogen?" she asked, clearly dumbfounded.

"And possibly Moll Brody," James replied softly.

Arabella took a step back, disbelief written on her face. "Imogen was my dearest friend. I would never have hurt her. And I barely know Moll Brody. I have only ever seen her in church. James, you must tell Inspector Haze the truth. I parted with Imogen in the woods and came to meet you here. I didn't follow her to the Gypsy campsite. I was with you at the time of her death."

She looked imploringly at James, who nodded but looked thoughtful. "Bella, if I tell Inspector Haze that we met, then your mother and brother will find out about our relationship and interfere with our plans."

"So you would rather I was suspected of murdering my sister-in-law?" Arabella asked, taking another step back from him.

"Of course not, but that clodhopper of an inspector has nothing. All we have to do is keep silent and proceed with our plans once things settle down."

Arabella paused. The alteration in her expression was barely noticeable, but it was enough to warn James that he'd made a mistake. He reached for her again, his walking stick pressing against her arm as he tried to reason with her.

"Bella, we'll get married like we planned. We'll be together," James said, smiling at her winsomely. Arabella looked utterly bewildered. "It'll be me and you against the world," he continued, "and there's nothing your mother or your brother will be able to do about it. We'll be happy. All you have to do is stay strong for a few more weeks."

"And bear up under the scrutiny of the police?" Bella asked, her nostrils flaring in anger. "Inspector Haze clearly knows Imogen and I argued and that she'd threatened me. That gives me a motive. And he'll say I had opportunity. I could have followed her to the camp and strangled her to protect my secret. If you won't give me an alibi, there's nothing to suggest that I didn't do exactly that."

"Bella, no one can prove that you are responsible. There's simply no evidence against you. People argue all the time; that doesn't mean they go on to murder each other."

"Sometimes they do," Arabella replied. "When they feel threatened or scared. And I was, James. Imogen could have spoiled everything."

James lifted his hand to stroke Bella's pale cheek. "Bella, I don't care what you've done. I'll always love you. As long as you keep denying any involvement, Haze can't pin anything on you. Just think of how happy we will be once this is over," he cajoled.

"Will you still be happy if my brother refuses to hand over my portion?" Arabella asked, her eyes narrowing as she studied James.

His hand fell away, but he wasn't giving up. "Harry will want to avoid scandal. He'll come around. You'll see. He wouldn't want his sister to suffer or live in penury."

But Arabella was no longer listening, suspicion dawning in her eyes. "You were upset when I told you of my row with Imogen. You said she had the power to ruin everything, then you left directly afterward. You said you had work to do," Arabella said quietly, pinning James with her light-blue stare. "Imogen was killed with a string," Arabella said quietly, as if talking to herself. Her head jerked upward as she stared at James in horror. "You had purchased new strings for your violin when you went to Brentwood. They were still in your pocket. The packet fell out when you took out your handkerchief to dry my tears," Arabella choked out. She took a hasty step back. "Oh God, it was you. You killed Imogen and that other woman."

James hesitated just long enough to give Arabella the answer she needed.

Her hand flew to her mouth. "Oh God. That's why you don't want to give me an alibi, because if I tell the inspector you left immediately after I told you of Imogen's threat, his suspicion will turn to you. How could I have been so blind?" she moaned.

"Bella, I did it for us," James cried. "Imogen would have ruined our lives. She was jealous that I loved you and not her. She didn't want us to be married."

"You stood there and said you loved me regardless of what I'd done, when all along, you knew the truth. But I can see why you did that. You wanted me to think that you love me so much, you wouldn't care if I had committed murder, binding me to you even tighter. Is it me you love, James, or my money?" she exclaimed, tears streaming down her cheeks.

"Bella, you've got it all wrong," James pleaded.

Arabella hunched her shoulders defensively, but her gaze was defiant, her chin jutting out as she confronted James, the words coming in a breathless torrent. "Imogen was warning me off. She said you were after my money, as you had been after hers. She said she was the one who'd rejected you, James, not the other way around, once she'd realized what you were truly after. And she'd been the perfect mark, hadn't she? Shy, unsure of herself, always just a little bit apart. All you had to do was show a little bit of interest, a little sympathy, and she was yours for the taking." Arabella drew in a shaky breath, her chest heaving with emotion. "Imogen tried to save me from making a horrible mistake, and she died because of it."

"Bella, what she told you was a lie. Imogen pursued me. She made my life a living hell. She was always there, hovering, talking about her feelings for me, begging me to run away with her."

Arabella shook her head. "Imogen would never have behaved that way, and you'd realize that if you had known her even a little. She might have fancied herself in love with you, but she would have never acted on it. She always intended to honor her commitment to Harry, even if she didn't love him. So, once she was married and out of your reach, you turned your sights on me. Poor Arabella. Humiliated, rejected, overlooked—the perfect target."

"Bella, I love you," James cried. "I committed the ultimate sin for you."

"You killed an innocent young woman who was carrying my brother's child. You snuffed out two lives—no, three, if you killed Moll Brody to protect your prospects."

"I never laid a hand on this Moll," James retorted. "I don't even know who she is." He no longer looked dejected. He was angry, and afraid. His plans were unraveling, and now Arabella had the power to see him hang for the murder of her friend.

"How did you do it, James? How did you lure her into that caravan?" Arabella demanded. She was calmer now, the stormy emotions of moments before replaced by cold reason and a desire to understand.

James shrugged. "I pretended to be ill and told her I needed to sit down. She helped me into the caravan. The door was facing away from the camp, so no one saw us. That silly dog barked a few times but then lost interest when it saw a squirrel. And even if it'd barked its head off, no one would have noticed. An argument broke out between two men, and there was all this shouting and gesticulating. It was the perfect cover."

"So, you killed her and left her there," Arabella said softly. "Like rubbish."

"She tried to turn you away from me," James said miserably. "I was devastated. I didn't know what I was doing."

"Oh, you knew," Arabella said. "And you were prepared to allow Inspector Haze to believe that I was the murderer." The disgust on her face seemed to stab him right through the heart. "I'm leaving. I never want to see you again, James. And don't worry, I won't give you away," Arabella spat out. "Not for your sake. For mine. Any association with you is bound to destroy my life if the truth comes out. So you're safe. For now. Inspector Haze is not as stupid as you seem to think. He'll figure it out, and then you'll hang."

Arabella spun on her heel and made to leave, but James Reed was faster. He swung his walking stick about and grabbed it with his other hand, pressing the shaft against Arabella's throat until her head was up against his chest, the stick cutting off oxygen and suffocating the young woman.

Arabella let out a strangled cry, struggling desperately to release the pressure on her throat, but James Reed only pressed harder. Arabella's attempts to free herself forced him to turn, and he leaned against the door, effectively cutting off any possible aid. Arabella's face turned bright red, then a dangerous shade of purple as she gasped for breath, her eyes bulging with lack of oxygen and the horror of what was happening. James Reed's mouth twisted into an evil grin as Arabella's resistance weakened.

"It's too bad, Bella," he hissed. "We could have been happy had you not been such a prig."

Daniel sprang toward the door to get to Arabella, but Jason had a different idea. He pulled out his gun and aimed. Thankfully, James Reed was considerably taller than Arabella, leaving his head unobstructed. Jason fired, hoping he wasn't so out of practice as to waste his one chance. The bullet whistled through the air, the acrid smell of gunpowder filling Jason's nose. It probably took only a second or two, but it felt like an eternity as Jason waited to see if his aim had been true.

James Reed's head jerked back, his hat falling backward as he loosened his hold on the stick and sagged against the door that Daniel was trying to open from the other side. Arabella shrieked and fell to her knees, grabbing at her throat and gasping for air, tears coursing down her cheeks as she coughed and wheezed. As soon as she got enough oxygen into her lungs, she turned her head, as though fearful of a second attempt on her life. Her hand flew to her mouth, and she heaved and emptied her stomach onto the walkway as she saw her lover, half sitting against the door, half lying on the walkway, a bullet hole between his eyes and blood trickling down the side of his nose and onto his chin. His eyes were wide open, a look of surprise on a face that had been extraordinarily handsome until only a moment ago.

Daniel finally managed to push the door open, and the body slid sideways as he forced his way in. He looked at the carnage, then sprang to Arabella's aid, lifting her to her feet and holding her close as she shivered violently, gut-wrenching sobs erupting from her heaving chest.

"It's all right. He's gone. He can't hurt you anymore," Daniel whispered. Arabella nodded into his shoulder but continued to weep, her arms wrapped tight around Daniel's middle as she pressed herself even closer to him.

Jason pushed the gun into the waistband of his trousers and walked around the side of the building, entering the boathouse just as Arabella drew back from Daniel and saw him, her eyes widening in surprise.

"It was you," she whispered, her wild gaze fixing on Jason. "You shot him."

"Yes."

Arabella released Daniel and hurled herself at Jason, wrapping her arms around his neck. "Thank you," she mumbled. "Oh, thank you, my lord. You saved my life."

"You needn't thank me," Jason said, a bit embarrassed as he held her away from him. "I'm glad you're all right."

Arabella's throat was a livid red but she was able to speak, so her larynx hadn't been crushed. There'd be no permanent damage.

"Daniel, shall I escort Miss Chadwick home?" Jason asked.

Arabella had calmed down somewhat, but the aftershock of what had happened was yet to come. She'd need understanding and care in the coming days, something he'd need to explain to Caroline, who was as likely to berate her as she was to comfort her.

"Of course. I'll see to the body," Daniel said. "Are you all right?" he asked, looking at Jason closely.

"Of course. Miss Chadwick," Jason said, offering Arabella his arm.

They walked out into the late afternoon, the sun gentle on their shoulders as they made their way toward the manor house and the explanations and recriminations that awaited poor Arabella.

"I thought he was a good man," Arabella said as they walked slowly down a wooded path. "I thought he loved me."

"Perhaps he did," Jason said, not wanting to make her feel worse than she already did.

"I think he only wanted my money. What a cad!" Arabella exclaimed.

Jason chose not to point out that most men she came across would want her money, only they probably wouldn't go so far as to kill for it. The only difference between James Reed and Lawrence

Foxley was that the latter had a title and estate to bargain with, unlike James Reed, who had to get along on the talents he'd been born with. Jason felt no remorse for killing the man. He'd have killed Arabella, then turned his sights on Tom Marin, who was the only other person to know that Arabella and James had met at the boathouse, as far as he knew. There was no knowing if he'd killed anyone before Imogen Chadwick, but he'd likely have killed again.

"You've done him a favor," Arabella said, her expression thoughtful beneath the brim of her bonnet.

"How so?" Jason asked. It was good that she was talking. It'd help her to deal with the aftermath of the trauma she'd just suffered.

"You gave him a quick, honorable death. Better to be shot between the eyes than to spend months in jail, have your name and reputation dragged through the mud, and then have to face your executioner. I don't think there can be anything more terrifying than walking to your own execution, knowing you're about to die in a horrible, possibly prolonged way. I'm glad you spared him that."

"Are you?" Jason asked, wondering if she'd have forgiven James Reed, given time.

"Yes. I did love him, you know. Perhaps it was all an act, but he made me feel seen, and loved. With James, I always felt special, and beautiful. He said all the right things, I suppose. Maybe because he'd said them so many times to those who came before me."

"There's no reason to suspect there had been any victims before Imogen," Jason said, wishing only to diminish her pain.

"I suppose I'll never know now, but I'll have to live with the knowledge that Imogen died because of me."

"You had no way of knowing that James Reed would murder Imogen."

"No, but I should have listened to her. Imogen didn't have a devious bone in her body. I should have realized she was telling me the truth, but I thought she was jealous of our love and wanted to destroy it so that I could have a marriage as dull and lifeless as hers. I said cruel things to her when I should have been thanking her for trying to save me. I'll never get to tell her that I'm sorry," Arabella said, her voice quivering.

"You can still tell her. I think she'll hear you."

"Do you? Do you think James will hear me if I tell him to rot in hell?"

"Probably. Give it a try," Jason said, smiling down at her. "It might make you feel better."

"You're a surprising man, Lord Redmond. Katherine is lucky to have your love."

"And I'm lucky to have hers."

Arabella looked up at him, smiling sadly. "Perhaps one day I'll meet a man who's truly worthy of my love."

"I'm sure you will. Just don't let anyone pressure you into marrying against your will. Wait for the right one."

"A girl doesn't have the luxury of time, my lord. If I don't marry soon, my chances of finding a husband will dwindle with every passing year. I will have to compete with younger girls who have an unblemished reputation, and I will come up wanting. No one wants a woman who's been jilted, tainted by scandal, and who's thought to be too picky. I will take whatever I can get and make the most of it."

"That's sensible," Jason replied, thinking it anything but.

He could understand her, though. As a man, he didn't have to rush or force himself to accept a marriage with a woman he didn't desire. It was different for women, especially in England, where the rules were more stringent. Arabella Chadwick wouldn't have many choices, especially if the truth of her affair with James Reed were to come out, and she knew that. Jason felt desperately sad for her as he escorted her to the door and used the knocker to announce their presence. He took a deep breath, striving for patience as Llewellyn opened the door. He wasn't looking forward to the explanations that were about to come.

Chapter 35

Three hours later, Jason and Daniel reconvened in Jason's drawing room. With the help of John Marin, Daniel had delivered James Reed's body to the Brentwood Police Station and had given DI Coleridge an account of what had occurred. An abridged version of events would be given to the press, who would publish the story without mentioning Arabella Chadwick by name. It was only right to try to salvage her reputation, given what she had endured at the hands of her lover.

Jason took a sip of his whisky and rested his head against the back of the wingchair, exhaling deeply. It had taken him nearly two hours to extricate himself from the Chadwicks, who had been in turns shocked, horrified, tearful, grateful, angry, and self-righteous. He had been glad when Arabella had finally been allowed to go up to her room, where she would no doubt have passed out on her bed after taking the laudanum Caroline had offered her.

"Will Arabella be all right?" Daniel asked.

"She will. In time. And so will the Romani. I've had a quiet word with Harry Chadwick regarding his nocturnal activities, and he will reimburse the Romani for the horses and the damage to their caravans. He's almost ashamed of himself, but not quite."

"I didn't think he would be, but I'm glad he's willing to compensate those poor people. Of course, he can't replace Borzo."

"No, he can't." Jason took another slow sip. "So, we now know what happened to Imogen and why, but we still have no inkling what became of Moll."

Daniel took a sip of his own drink. "I think I have an idea of where Moll is."

"Do you?"

"It's just a hunch, so I'm not ready to share it just yet."

"All right," Jason said. He was too tired to cajole Daniel into sharing his theory. "Will you stay for dinner?"

"No, thank you. I want to go home and see my girls," Daniel said, a silly grin spreading across his normally serious face. "I tell you, Jason, there's no feeling like that of holding your own child. You forget everything in the world but the needs of that tiny person. I feel like I've loved Charlotte forever, and she's only been here for a day."

Jason felt a pang of longing at Daniel's words. He was nearly thirty. He was more than ready for children of his own, and he hoped Katherine was too. Perhaps by this time next year…

"Well, I'll push off," Daniel said, rising to his feet. "Have a good night, my friend."

"And you," Jason said, seriously considering skipping dinner and just heading up to bed.

"I'll collect you tomorrow, around nine," Daniel said.

Jason nodded. He didn't bother to ask where they were going. He'd find out soon enough, but he was fairly certain it wasn't to church.

Chapter 36

Sunday, May 12

Morning came quickly. Jason washed and dressed, gulped down a cup of coffee, then drank a second cup more slowly with his breakfast, and stepped outside, ready to meet Daniel when he arrived. Punctual as ever, Daniel appeared at a few minutes to nine, looking as tired as he had last night.

"Charlotte isn't sleeping well?" Jason asked as he climbed in next to Daniel.

"Charlotte is sleeping like the proverbial baby; it's I who can't sleep. My mind kept going over the case all night, wondering if I'm right about Moll," Daniel said. "I was up with the birds this morning."

"Perhaps you should take a few days off once this case is wrapped up. You could do with a rest," Jason suggested.

"I think I just might."

Jason was surprised when they drove into the village and Daniel stopped the cart in front of the Red Stag. He tossed the reins to Matty Locke and beckoned for Jason to follow him inside.

Davy was in the taproom, a less-than-clean apron wrapped around his middle, broom in hand as he swept the floor. He glanced up in surprise as the two men entered.

"What can I do for ye, gents?" Davy asked, a wary look passing over his features.

"I'd like to speak to Moll," Daniel said. "I have some questions to put to her."

Davy blanched, his eyes sliding away from the two men. "She ain't 'ere, guv. Ye know that."

"Do I?" Daniel asked. "Come on, Davy. The murder has been solved. Lord Redmond put a bullet between the eyes of the killer. It's safe for Moll to come out now."

"The killer is dead?" Davy asked, his eyebrows lifting in surprise. "Who was it?"

"Squire Talbot's estate manager. I reckon you'll read about it in the papers this morning," Daniel said. "Tell Moll it's safe to come out."

Davy nodded, set aside the broom, and headed for the door that led to the cellar. "Moll, come on out, love," he called out.

A few moments later, Moll emerged from the cellar, squinting at the bright light streaming through the leaded windows. Moll looked tired and a bit unkempt but otherwise unharmed.

"Good morning, Moll. We'd like a word," Daniel said.

Moll walked over to a window table and sat down, turning her face up to the light as if she'd been incarcerated for years.

"The killer is dead. You're safe," Daniel said as he took a seat across from her, followed by Jason, who was impressed by Daniel's detective skills.

Moll took a deep breath and allowed her shoulders to sag in relief. "I'm sorry for the trouble I caused, but I were scared," Moll said, her eyes searching Daniel's for understanding.

"So, the search for Moll was a ruse?" Daniel demanded, nailing Davy, who'd sat down next to Moll, with his disapproving gaze.

"It weren't," Davy protested. "I really thought she were gone."

"Tell us what happened," Jason invited, acting the peacemaker.

Moll sighed. "I went for a walk with Tristan Carmichael on Tuesday afternoon. It were a lovely day, and 'e were so nice." She smiled at the memory. "'E gave me a keepsake." She held out her hand, showing them a silver ring with a red stone, probably a ruby, and smiling happily. "Tristan had to get back to town, so I went off to the Gypsy camp. I wanted to say 'ow-ye-do," Moll explained. "I visit every year."

"What happened then?" Daniel asked.

"As I approached the camp, I saw the door of the green caravan—that's Luca's vardo—open. A man stood in the doorway, the one as works for the squire. I didn't know 'is name. There were blood on 'is gloves, and 'e 'ad this wild-eyed look in 'is eyes. 'E clutched a bloodied string in 'is 'ands. Our eyes met, and I suddenly knew that I'd seen something I shouldn't. He stepped forward. It were then that I saw the body, the blood glistening on the floor when the light 'it it just so.

I froze, unsure what to do, and that's when 'e lurched forward, 'is teeth bared, the string stretched between 'is 'ands. I ran. I were so scared," Moll said, her eyes filling with tears. "I just knew that if 'e caught me, 'e'd kill me too."

"But he didn't catch up to you?" Daniel asked.

"'E chased me as far as the road, but then 'e fell back. I s'pose 'e were afraid someone would come along. But there were no one. I were alone. I ran all the way back to the village and 'id in Mrs. Etty's shed, ye know the one where she lays out the dead. No one would ever go in there, not willingly anyway. I thought if I go back to the Stag, 'e'll know where to find me, and 'e'll come for me. So I stayed in the shed all night, trying to figure out what to do."

"And you decided to disappear until the murderer was apprehended?" Jason asked, trying to imagine Moll's terror as she hid in the Dead Shed, as the place was known.

Moll nodded. "I didn't want to tell Davy. 'E'd try to convince me I were safe at the Stag, but I weren't, not as long as 'e knew where to find me, and I were too afraid to tell ye 'e's done for Imogen," Moll said tearfully. "I 'eard Estelle Etty say it were Imogen when she spoke to 'er neighbor over the fence. So, I sneaked into the cellar when everyone were out looking for me," she confessed. "I stayed there, all quiet-like, 'oping ye'd catch 'im and I could come out."

"And then Davy found you," Daniel concluded. "And told you to stay down there a little while longer, just until it was safe to come out." Moll nodded.

"How'd ye know?" Davy asked. "How'd ye guess she were safe?"

"I've met people whose loved ones have gone missing. They have this haunted look in their eyes, this desperate hope that not all is lost and the person will be returned to them. You didn't look like a haunted man, Davy. You looked tired and upset, but not haunted or grieving. You looked furtive, and I wager you wouldn't have let me into your cellar. Once you discovered Moll was there, you agreed to keep her secret."

"I told 'er she should come out and speak to ye," Davy said, crossing his arms defensively. "I told 'er ye'd keep 'er safe, but she were too frightened after what she'd seen. She didn't want to take the chance. Thought 'e'd strangle 'er when she went to the privy or climb into 'er room at night. She were right, though, weren't she?" Davy asked, tilting his head. "Ye found 'im out, and Moll is safe."

"We'd have found him sooner had you told us what you'd seen," Jason pointed out.

Moll nodded. "I should 'ave, but I didn't know 'is name, nor did I know if 'e were still there, at the squire's 'ouse. While ye looked for 'im, 'e could 'ave done for me too."

"Well, Tristan will be relieved to hear you're safe," Daniel said, a bit sarcastically. "Perhaps he could have protected you."

"Tristan is not a bad sort," Moll said, crossing her arms just like her uncle. "'E ain't like his da. 'E's kind and gentle."

Davy snorted, but turned the snort into a cough when Moll glared at him.

"You'll have to make an official statement," Daniel said.

"And thank the men who spent hours combing the countryside for you," Jason added, deeply annoyed with Moll for withholding vital information.

"I will. It were nice to know 'ow much everyone cared," Moll said, tearing up again. "Everyone was so kind."

"I'm glad you're safe and sound, Moll," Daniel said, rising to his feet.

"I think a celebration is in order," Davy said. "Free drinks for everyone tonight. I hope you both come," he said, looking from Daniel to Jason.

"I know I will," Jason said, and nudged Daniel.

"I suppose I can pop in for one drink," Daniel said grudgingly. He was clearly upset with Moll for not coming forward but happy to see her unharmed.

"See ye tonight, lads," Moll said, her irrepressible smile returning. For a moment, she looked just like Zamfira.

"All's well that ends well, I suppose," Daniel grumbled as they left the tavern. "I'm going home to have a kip."

"I'm going to pay a call on my fiancée," Jason replied, smiling at the prospect. "She'll want to hear all the details. She always does."

"Bloodthirsty woman," Daniel joked as he climbed into the dogcart.

"That's how I like them," Jason replied, and walked off with a casual wave.

Epilogue

Saturday, June 1

The smell of orange blossoms and beeswax polish were heavy on the air, and arrows of sunlight streamed through the stained-glass windows of St. Catherine's. Having approached the altar, Jason turned around so that he could watch his bride walk down the aisle on the arm of Squire Talbot, who'd been prevailed upon to give his niece away since her father was to perform the ceremony.

The squire was dressed in a dark-gray suit and wore a black cravat, as mourning etiquette required, but no respectful attire could compete with the sadness in his eyes. He had only just given away Imogen in marriage, never suspecting that he'd be walking behind her casket a few short months later. Still, he had been willing to come out of mourning for one day to honor Jason and Katherine, who'd been instrumental in bringing the killer to justice.

Jason glanced at Micah, who stood next to him, wearing a new suit and looking very dapper. He looked tense, conscious of his responsibility as best man and patting his pocket every few seconds to assure himself Katherine's wedding ring was still there. The bride's side of the church was nearly full—Katherine was much admired and respected in the community—but the groom's side only held a dozen people. The pews were occupied by Redmond Hall staff, Mary, Shawn Sullivan, and, of course, Daniel, Sarah, and Harriet, who dabbed at her eyes, overcome with emotion, even though the wedding hadn't started yet. Arabella Chadwick, who'd chosen to sit apart from her family, occupied a seat in the first pew.

Just across from her, Caroline Chadwick sat with her back erect, her black gown severe. Her family had suffered a terrible blow, but Caroline Chadwick would rally. She was a survivor, just like her children. Harry had chosen not to come, out of respect for Imogen, but Lucinda was there next to Caroline, her gaze fixed on something just beyond Jason's shoulder. She looked demure and wraithlike in her mourning gown, possibly because Sir Lawrence was in attendance and she needed to play the part of the grieving sister-in-law. Sir Lawrence loosely held Lucinda's hand, his gaze adoring as he checked on her from time to time. Perhaps Lucinda stood a chance of a happy marriage with a man who clearly adored her, and not only for her money. Jason hoped Arabella would find someone who'd care for her as well. She deserved it after what she'd been through.

Daniel gave Jason an encouraging smile as the church doors opened and the organ began to play. Jason was glad Daniel understood his decision to ask Micah to stand up for him. Daniel was a friend, a confidant, and a colleague, but Micah had been there when Jason was at his lowest and to some degree had given him a reason to live, as had the search for Mary. She'd decided to stay in England until the end of the summer, by which time Micah would be faced with a decision of his own.

As the squire and Katherine approached the altar, Jason smiled at his bride, clearing his mind of all thoughts but those of her. This day had been a long time coming, but it was here, and he was incandescently happy. Katherine took her place next to him, and their eyes met as she gazed up at him, radiant in her joy. There would be ups and downs, elation and grief but today was all about love.

The End

Please turn the page for an excerpt from Murder in the Grave A Redmond and Haze Mystery Book 5

Notes

I hope you've enjoyed this installment of the Redmond and Haze mysteries and will check out future books.

I'd love to hear your thoughts and suggestions. I can be found at irina.shapiro@yahoo.com, www.irinashapiroauthor.com, or https://www.facebook.com/IrinaShapiro2/.

If you would like to join my Victorian mysteries mailing list, please use this link.

https://landing.mailerlite.com/webforms/landing/u9d9o2

An Excerpt from Murder in the Grave
A Redmond and Haze Mystery Book 5

Prologue

The day dawned bright and humid, the sun blazing in a cloudless sky and the temperature rising with every passing hour. The worst kind of day for a funeral, Arthur Weeks reflected as he entered the cemetery and walked toward the grave he'd dug yesterday. It was bad enough to bury someone in pouring rain or biting cold, but to stand beside an open grave in black, often woolen mourning attire while the sun beat down mercilessly on one's head and shoulders was as near to hell as Arthur could imagine. He would take a crisp autumn day over the heat of summer any day.

There was no need for Arthur to check on the grave, but he liked to make sure everything was ready for the burial, nonetheless. He was a conscientious man who took his responsibilities seriously. The graveyard at St. Martin's was neat and tidy, the weeds pulled, the flowers watered, and the grass cut. Arthur often spoke to the dead as he went about his duties, calling them by name, especially since he'd known so many of them in life. He told them about his days and the happenings in the village, desperate for someone to talk to since his wife had joined the ranks of his deceased friends nearly five years ago now.

Approaching the grave, Arthur frowned in consternation. When he'd finished digging the grave, the sides had been straight, the corners sharp, and the mound of earth piled on the side had been a neat brown hillock just waiting to be returned to its proper place once the coffin had been lowered into the ground. This morning, the hillock was considerably smaller and one of the sides of the grave looked ragged, as if someone had stood at the very edge and rocked back and forth, undoing all his hard work. Striding toward the grave, Arthur yanked the shovel he'd left nearby and was just about to fix the edge to make sure it looked right and proper when something struck him as odd.

The grave wasn't deep enough. Arthur peered in, unsure what to do. Had he made a mistake in his measurements? Was there time to dig another two feet before the funeral? He was already dressed in his best suit, his only suit, and he didn't want to be covered in dirt when the mourners arrived. Nevertheless, the grave had to be six feet deep, and it was his responsibility to ensure that everything was up to snuff.

Arthur removed his coat, hung it over a nearby headstone, and jumped into the grave, ready to rectify his mistake.

He was about to drive the shovel into the rich earth when his gaze fell on something long and pale sticking out of the ground. A root? Arthur bent down and grabbed the offending piece of wood, ready to yank it from the soil. He let out a shrill cry as he found himself holding on to a cold, stiff finger that was still attached to a hand. Being made of sterner stuff than most, Arthur took a moment to collect himself, then used his hands to clear away the dirt from the person's face. Wide blue eyes met Arthur's gaze, a grimace of pain etched into the man's bloodied face. Arthur took a step back, his heart hammering in his breast.

"Dear God," he whispered as he looked heavenward, hoping for guidance. He'd seen many a dead body in his sixty-five years, but he'd never seen anything like this.

Chapter 1

Tuesday, August 6, 1867

Jason Redmond came awake in the best way possible to find his new wife leaning over him, her lips brushing against his as her nightdress offered a tantalizing glimpse of her lovely breasts. He wrapped his arms around her and returned her kiss, ready and willing to perform his husbandly duties until his bride was satisfied. His plans were unexpectedly thwarted when Katherine suddenly pulled away, her hand flying to her mouth as she jumped out of bed and ran for the newly installed water closet, slamming the door behind her.

So, it's like that, is it? Jason thought, smiling happily despite his disappointment at having to forgo making love to his bride.

Katherine emerged a few minutes later, looking pale and ill. "I'm sorry," she moaned. "I must have eaten something that didn't agree with me last night."

Jason came toward her and took her in his arms, holding her close.

"Do you feel unwell?" Katherine asked, studying his face. She looked heartbreakingly vulnerable without her spectacles and with her hair tumbling down her back, a different person to the calm, composed Katherine, whose hair was always modestly arranged and her glasses perched on her pert nose, magnifying her dark eyes.

"I'm well, Katie. In fact, I'm better than well," Jason said, taking her face in his hands.

"Are you?" Katherine said, looking at him earnestly. "Well, that's something, I suppose."

"Do you feel any better?" Jason asked as the color began to return to her face.

"A little. Perhaps a cup of tea will set me to rights. I think it was that creamed veal Mrs. Dodson made last night. It really was too rich."

"Katie—"

"I'll tell her not to make it again," Katherine said, the look of determination returning now that she felt marginally better. "I really do prefer lighter fare, especially so close to bedtime." Katherine gently removed Jason's hands and glanced at the window. "I suppose I had better get dressed. It looks to be a fine day outside. I promised I'd visit Father this morning."

"Katie—" Jason tried again.

"Yes, I know I was at the vicarage only a few days ago, but he does get lonely. He likes me to read over his sermons, and it's my turn to arrange the church flowers."

"Katie—"

"Yes, my dear?" Katherine asked, focusing on him once again.

"You haven't had your courses since we were in Rome," Jason pointed out gently.

"Haven't I?" she asked, blushing prettily. This was not the kind of thing she felt comfortable discussing, even though he was a doctor and knew all about the female body, at least in theory.

"And this is the third time this week you've felt unwell," Jason continued.

Her mouth dropped open and her eyes widened in shock, the true meaning of his words finally sinking in. "Oh, my word!" she exclaimed, grabbing his hand. "Do you think…?"

"I think it's a very good possibility given how often we—" He never got to finish the sentence.

There was an urgent knock on the door, followed by Dodson, who colored with embarrassment when he saw Katherine in a state of undress.

"I beg your pardon, my lord, my lady. You're wanted, sir. Urgently."

"What happened?" Jason asked, wishing more than anything that whatever it was hadn't happened today of all days, or had at least waited for an hour or two so that he could spend some time with Katie. She was sure to have questions or, at the very least, require his support at such a momentous moment in their lives.

"There's a body, sir. In a grave. Constable Pullman is downstairs," Dodson added, his disapproval evident.

Dodson didn't enjoy having the police invade Redmond Hall every time there was a suspicious death, and didn't bother to hide his opinion that no nobleman should involve himself in solving crimes, and worse yet, perform autopsies on the deceased in the basement mortuary of the Brentwood police station. But Jason Redmond was no ordinary nobleman, nor had he been raised in England, where duty and a sense of propriety would have been hammered into him since birth. Despite his proud lineage, Jason had been born and raised in America, had trained as a surgeon, and had fought in the American Civil War, the scars of that conflict still fresh on his heart, if no longer on his body. He had resigned himself to claiming his inheritance but wasn't prepared to give up medicine or the need to feel useful and intellectually stimulated. He loved a challenge, eager to solve the puzzle using nothing but his wits and gut instinct. And as long as Katherine took no issue with his desire to assist the police, he would continue to do so.

"Tell Constable Pullman I'll be right down," Jason said. "Katie, will you be all right on your own for a few hours?" he asked, feeling like a cad for leaving her.

"Of course I'll be all right," Katherine said as she reached for her spectacles and slid them onto her nose, her gaze now more focused. "Jason, are you pleased?" she asked, her voice small and unsure.

"I'm thrilled to bits," Jason said, and pulled her to him, giving her a sound kiss. "And I will show you just how happy I am when I return. In the meantime, have a light breakfast and go for a walk before it gets too hot."

"Doctor's orders?" Katherine asked, her earnest expression bringing out his every protective instinct.

"Husband's orders," Jason replied, stroking her cheek. "I wish I didn't have to leave you. I'm sorry."

"You don't have anything to apologize for, and I wouldn't have you any other way. Now, go. A body won't keep long in this heat."

"I love you, darlin'," Jason said, putting on an exaggerated American accent that always made her laugh.

"I love you too, Yank," Katherine replied, flashing him an impish grin.

Chapter 2

Jason jumped down from the police wagon driven by Constable Pullman and followed him into the graveyard, where Inspector Daniel Haze was waiting impatiently, his hands clasped behind his back, his face tight with displeasure. Ned Hollingsworth, the police photographer, was leaning against a gravestone, a cheroot dangling from the side of his mouth, his expression radiating irritation as he awaited his opportunity to photograph the victim. His camera was already set up, the tripod positioned several feet from the open grave in order to get a closeup once the body was lifted out. The police called him when there was a particularly puzzling or gruesome case that required photographic evidence, and Ned, a weasel of a man, had a sideline of selling copies of crime-scene photos to the newspapers, which was probably more profitable.

Inspector Haze seemed to relax marginally when he spotted Jason and raised his hand in greeting, clearly relieved to be able to get on with the morning's work. Ned Hollingsworth tipped his hat and continued to smoke.

"Jason, thank you for coming so quickly," Daniel said as Jason approached the open grave and stared down into its depths, his eyebrows lifting in astonishment at the sight that greeted him. It was gruesome, and unexpectedly disturbing because the victim appeared to be staring directly at him, his blue gaze full of accusation, his face crusted with blood, and the split skull already crawling with maggots.

Jason looked away. "Have you examined the surrounding area?" he asked Daniel.

"I have. The side of the grave had been disturbed. I believe the victim had been standing at the edge, or close to it, just before falling backward, probably driven over by the force of the blow. The killer used some of the dug-up soil to cover the corpse. Had the gravedigger not come by this morning to check on his work, the coffin would have been lowered into the grave, and the body would never have been discovered."

"Were there no footprints?" Jason asked.

"I think there must have been, but they were obliterated when the soil was disturbed. There's blood on the shovel, which belongs to Mr. Weeks and has been here since he dug the grave yesterday. Would you like to examine the corpse inside the grave, or would you like it lifted out?" Daniel asked.

"I want the body shifted onto a wooden panel and lifted out carefully, so as to preserve as much of the original damage as possible."

"Understood," Daniel said. "Constable Pullman, please assist Mr. Weeks in retrieving the body."

Constable Pullman groaned but didn't argue, knowing it to be useless. Someone had to do the grunt work, and it was usually him. He removed his helmet and set it on one of the neighboring graves, then turned to the gravedigger, who'd already brought a narrow wooden panel that might have been part of an old door, and two lengths of thick rope.

"How shall we go about this?" Constable Pullman asked, his reluctance to get into the grave obvious.

"I will go down there, shift the body onto the plank, then run the rope beneath the wood. Then we will use the ropes to lift 'im. You needn't go down there, Constable," Arthur Weeks said.

"Well, go on, then," Constable Pullman said, his relief palpable.

Arthur Weeks lowered himself into the grave and went about arranging the body while the four men looked on, each ready to do his bit. It took less than ten minutes to lift the body out of the grave, at which point everyone stood aside to allow Ned Hollingsworth to take his photographs. Once finished, he closed the lens, detached the camera from the tripod and set is on the ground, then folded the tripod and stuffed it under his arm before picking up the camera and striding off, his presence no longer required. He would return to Brentwood with Constable Pullman and retire to his darkroom, where he would develop the photographs and deliver them to the station, probably no later than noon tomorrow.

"Do you think he was dead when he went in?" Daniel asked as Jason bent over the body.

"I hope so, but I can't be certain until I perform a postmortem," Jason replied. "He was struck on the head with something hard and sharp, most likely the shovel you found," Jason said, examining the head wound that had nearly cleaved the man's skull as if it were a ripe melon. Rigor mortis had already begun to set in, and the presence of maggots confirmed Jason's suspicion that the man had been in that hole for at least twelve hours.

"He doesn't appear to have any other injuries, but there's dirt under his fingernails," Jason said, lifting the man's hand to show Daniel.

Daniel nodded. "Let's get him to the mortuary. I don't think there's anything more we can do here. Constable, get him into the wagon," Daniel instructed.

"Yes, sir."

Constable Pullman and Arthur Weeks hefted the wooden panel and carried the body to the police wagon, which was parked just beyond the lychgate. Ned Hollingsworth was already perched on the bench.

"I'd like to complete the postmortem within the next few hours. I need to get home," Jason added anxiously.

"Is everything all right?" Daniel asked, truly looking at Jason for the first time. "You seem a bit distracted."

"Everything is fine. It's just that Katherine wasn't feeling well this morning. I want to check on her."

"The postmortem can wait until tomorrow," Daniel suggested with some reluctance.

"I'd rather do it now. It's too hot to leave the body lying around for too long. I'll have answers for you by this afternoon," Jason said, and tipped his hat. "We'll talk later."

He strode toward the wagon and climbed into the back, grateful that the victim's body had been covered with a length of filthy sackcloth. At the very least, it would keep the flies away. Jason leaned against the side of the wagon and closed his eyes, his mind turning to more pleasant thoughts than the postmortem he was about to perform.

Chapter 3

Having seen the wagon off, Daniel returned to the graveyard and entered the church, which was marginally cooler, its dim confines a welcome respite from the blazing sunshine outside. The vicar sat in the front pew, his shoulders hunched, his head pulled in like that of a turtle. He was an elderly man with wispy white hair combed over his balding pate and a narrow, wrinkled face with a thin, hooked nose and light blue eyes. His cheeks were damp, either with sweat or tears; Daniel couldn't tell.

"Do you feel up to answering a few questions, Reverend Hodges?" he asked, sitting down next to the old man.

The vicar nodded sadly. "Yes, of course. Anything I can do to help."

"What time was the funeral scheduled for this morning?"

"Eleven o'clock. It was for Mrs. Crowe."

"Did she die of natural causes?" Daniel asked. The cause of Mrs. Crowe's death wasn't relevant at the moment, but that could change once he had more information to work with.

"Yes. She was ninety-six and had outlived half her children. I've asked Mr. Weeks to inform the family that the funeral is postponed until further notice."

"Thank you. That was good thinking on your part," Daniel said. "Did you know the deceased?" The vicar had been present at the gravesite when Daniel had arrived nearly two hours ago and had seen the body in all its gruesome glory.

The vicar's shoulders slumped even lower. "Yes. I knew him. It's Sebastian Slade, the curate."

"The curate?" Daniel wondered if he'd heard correctly.

"Yes. Mr. Slade had only just come to Upper Finchley. He'd been here less than a fortnight. I can't begin to image why anyone would want to do him harm. He was such a pleasant young man, so unassuming in his manner."

"Is it common to have a curate?" Daniel asked. St. Catherine's in Birch Hill, where Daniel had worshipped since he was a boy, had never had a curate.

"I'm getting on in years, and the duties of a parish priest are becoming onerous," Reverend Hodges explained. "I'm ready to retire, truth be told. Bishop Garner has assigned Mr. Slade to the parish with a view to him possibly taking over once he's completed his training."

"Was he not trained?" Daniel asked. He knew little of the inner workings of the Church.

"Mr. Slade graduated from the seminary just over a year ago. It's customary for a novice clergyman to serve as a curate for four years before becoming a full-fledged incumbent. Usually, the four years are done in the same position, but Mr. Slade had some sort of difficulty at his last posting and was transferred to Upper Finchley, as something of a punishment, I think," the vicar added.

"Why would that be a punishment?"

"Because Mr. Slade was from London and had hoped to find a permanent position at one of the many churches there. He wasn't overly fond of the country. He said so himself."

"I see. And has anything unusual happened since Mr. Slade's arrival? Had he had any arguments with anyone?" Daniel asked.

"No. He was so kind and self-effacing. Everyone liked him."

"Surely someone didn't," Daniel said, the face of the deceased appearing unbidden before Daniel's eyes and making him flinch.

Reverend Hodges shook his head. "I wish I knew who it was."

"Have there been any strangers in the village in the past few days?"

"No. Upper Finchley is not a coaching stop, and The Black Boar does not have rooms to let, so unless someone was staying with a relative or a friend, there'd be nowhere for them to lay their head. And, as far as I know, no one has had any visitors of late."

"I see."

"I do think you should speak to my wife. Edith is way more observant than I am, and she's an excellent judge of character. She's at home now, at the vicarage."

"Thank you. I will. And where would I find Bishop Garner?" Daniel asked before taking his leave.

"The bishop has an office in Chelmsford, but he resides in Brentwood. Number ten, Ingrave Road, if I'm not mistaken. You will keep me informed, won't you, Inspector?" Reverend Hodges asked. His manner had gone from shocked bereavement to stoic resignation during the course of the conversation.

"Of course," Daniel promised, eager to get going. There was nothing more to learn here.

The vicarage had seen better days, much like its occupants. Mrs. Hodges looked careworn and utterly colorless, her gray hair an almost perfect match to her dove-gray gown. She invited Daniel in and offered him tea, but the thought of drinking hot liquid on a day like today made him break out in a sheen of sweat. He was sweltering in his tweed suit and bowler hat.

"If I might have a cup of water, I'd be most grateful," Daniel said, wiping his forehead with his handkerchief.

"Of course. How about a nice glass of lemonade?"

"Yes, please," Daniel replied as he sat down on the worn settee.

Having drained the glass of lemonade without really tasting it, he turned his attention to Mrs. Hodges. "Your husband said that Mr. Slade was a pleasant, self-effacing young man. Do you share that view?"

"Oh, yes. Mr. Slade was a dear, dear man." She dabbed at her eyes and sniffled. "I just don't understand. Who would do such a dreadful thing? He didn't even know anyone here, not well enough to have offended, at any rate."

"Had he met everyone in the parish?" Daniel asked.

"He'd met most people, I should think. He took the service last Sunday since Neville—that's my husband—wasn't feeling well. He was very eloquent."

"Might he have said something that could be deemed offensive?" Daniel tried again.

"Oh, no. Nothing like that."

"Did anyone make any remarks after the service? Perhaps single someone out?"

"Not that I saw. Everyone seemed to have enjoyed the sermon. Mr. Slade was so pleased," Mrs. Hodges said. She looked utterly perplexed.

"And did anything unusual happen before, during, or after the service?" Daniel asked, hope quickly fading that he'd learn something of interest.

"One couple left during the service. Their child was fussing, so they took the poor mite home. I think he was unwell."

"I see. And did Mr. Slade reside here at the vicarage?"

"Oh, no. He lodged with Mrs. Monk. She's been taking in lodgers since her husband passed a few years back."

"Did Mr. Slade have to pay for his own lodgings?" Daniel asked.

"The expense would have been covered by the Church," Mrs. Hodges explained.

"Your husband mentioned that Mr. Slade's first position didn't work out. Did he say anything to you about what happened?"

"He just said there was some unpleasantness. A woman, most like. He was an attractive man," Mrs. Hodges said, dabbing at her eyes again. "What a waste of a young life."

"Yes," Daniel agreed. "It certainly is. Mrs. Hodges, were there any strangers in the village that you know of? Maybe someone had come for Mrs. Crowe's funeral," he suggested.

Mrs. Hodges shook her head. "Not that I can think of. Wait, no. There's Beth Lundy. She arrived in the village about a month ago, but she's not really a stranger. Born and bred in the village."

"And where has she come from?"

"She was working as a housekeeper in Chelmsford these forty years, but she finally saw fit to retire. Her sister was widowed last year, so she moved in with her. It's nice to have a bit of companionship in one's twilight years."

"Anyone else?"

"No, definitely not. This is a small village, Inspector. A stranger in our midst is not easily overlooked."

"Thank you, Mrs. Hodges."

"Happy to help," Mrs. Hodges replied, and pushed to her feet, ready to see him out.

Daniel left the vicarage and went to call on Mrs. Monk, who was waiting for him on her front step, eager to say her piece.

Mrs. Monk was considerably younger than Mrs. Hodges. In her late forties, Daniel estimated. She wore a becoming gown in a dusky shade of blue with a cameo brooch pinned to the bodice. Her hair was parted in the middle and wound into a neat bun at the back, but on her, the style didn't look severe, simply practical. Her light blue eyes were red-rimmed, which led Daniel to believe that she already knew the identity of the victim and was moved enough to mourn him.

"Please, come in, Inspector," Mrs. Monk said, opening the door and inviting him to go first. "Will you take a dish of tea?"

"No, thank you, Mrs. Monk. I'm rather warm," Daniel confessed.

"I think this has been one of the hottest summers of my life," she agreed. "A cup of ale, then?"

Despite having just had lemonade, Daniel accepted with alacrity and took the seat Mrs. Monk offered. The house was cozy and tastefully decorated, the furnishings and carpets in good condition, the curtains not yet faded. There were several stuffed birds displayed in glass cases, and needlepoint samplers of inspirational quotes hanging on the walls.

Mrs. Monk brought Daniel a cup of ale and settled in a chair across from him, watching him eagerly as he took a sip.

Daniel set the cup down and took out his notebook. "How well did you know Mr. Slade, Mrs. Monk?"

"As well as you can come to know someone in a fortnight," she replied.

"What was Mr. Slade like?"

"Earnest, polite, and surprisingly kind," Mrs. Monk said, her eyes welling up.

"How was he kind to you?" Daniel asked. Did the man have no flaws to work with?

"I've had a number of lodgers since my husband passed. They were civil and well-mannered men, but not one of them took the time to talk to me, to make me feel like a friend rather than just their skivvy. Mr. Slade was different. He treated me, not like his mother exactly, but more like a beloved aunt. He enjoyed my company," she said softly. "It's been rather a long time since anyone has made me feel like that."

"What did you talk about?"

"Books, music, art. Life," she added.

"And did he mention anyone who might wish to do him harm?"

"No, not at all."

"Did he tell you about his last posting?" Daniel asked.

"No, we didn't talk about that."

"Was there anything, anything at all, that you might describe as suspicious?" Daniel tried, desperate for something to go on.

Mrs. Monk considered the question. "Well, he did seem upset when he came home from church on Sunday. Something was on his mind."

"Did he tell you what?"

"No. He excused himself and went up to his room. Didn't even eat luncheon. He asked for a tray in his room at suppertime and went out early the next morning. Said he had some letters to post and wanted to make sure they went out that very day."

"Do you know whom he'd written to?" Daniel asked.

"I only saw the topmost letter. It was to his sister."

"Do you know the lady's name?" Daniel asked, hoping he'd have something to write down on the blank page.

"Yes. Mrs. Iris Holloway."

"And how many letters were there, Mrs. Monk?"

"There were three or four in total, I think," she replied.

"Did you see or hear Mr. Slade leave the house on Monday evening?"

Mrs. Monk shook her head. "My room is upstairs, but Mr. Slade's room is on the ground floor. If he'd gone out after I had retired for the night, I wouldn't have heard him unless he made a racket."

"And what time do you normally retire, Mrs. Monk?" Daniel asked.

"Around nine. I read for about a half hour, and then it's lights out. I'm a sound sleeper too," she added with an embarrassed smile. "My husband always said the house could burn around my ears and I'd never wake."

"Was the front door locked when you got up on Tuesday morning?"

Mrs. Monk looked thoughtful for a moment. "To be honest, I don't recall. I was in the kitchen preparing breakfast when I heard the commotion. That was after Mr. Weeks had found the body and raised the alarm, you understand. So I ran outside to see what was happening. Now that you mention it, I don't remember unlocking the door, but at the time, I might have thought that Mr. Slade had unlocked it first. I didn't know it was him who had died yet," she added, her eyes misting with tears.

"Mrs. Monk, may I see Mr. Slade's room?" Daniel asked as he stepped into the corridor, followed by the landlady.

"Yes, of course. It's just there," she said, pointing toward a door at the end of the corridor. "It's not locked."

Daniel entered the room and looked around. It was spacious and bright, with a window that overlooked the back garden and a freshly painted window frame and door. Blue-and-white wallpaper patterned with large, leafy flowers and vines matched the blue of the bed's coverlet and the curtains, which looked fairly new, the fabric not yet faded. A slightly worn carpet lay in the middle of the floor. There was a small writing desk facing the window, a matching chair, and a chest of drawers decorated with a crisp doily topped with a vase of wildflowers.

"I spruced up the room a bit after my Elliott died," Mrs. Monk explained. "For the lodgers," she added. Daniel took that to mean that this gave her leave to charge a higher price, but he couldn't say he blamed her. It was a pleasant room where a stranger might feel at home.

Daniel opened the drawers one by one. There were clean cotton drawers, shirts, and hose, and a neatly folded tweed suit and black tie, but not much else. He then turned his attention to the desk. Besides the usual writing implements, there were three books, all theologically themed, and a book of poems. There were no letters, photographs, or a diary, and no handwritten notes for a sermon.

"Is anything missing, Mrs. Monk?" Daniel asked, wondering if Sebastian Slade might have at least brought a photograph or a few keepsakes, given that he was in Upper Finchley to stay.

"No, that's just how he had it. He brought hardly anything with him. Said he liked to travel light."

"I see," Daniel said, taking one last look at the room. It was highly impersonal and told him little of the man, other than that he liked order and minimalism.

"Thank you," Daniel said, and turned to leave.

"You will find whoever did this, won't you, Inspector?" Mrs. Monk asked. "This terrible crime can't go unpunished."

"I will do everything in my power to apprehend the killer, Mrs. Monk."

She looked at him, her gaze intense, her mouth slightly parted as their eyes met. Daniel wondered if Sebastian Slade might have been more affectionate to his landlady than Mrs. Monk was letting on but decided not to ask, not unless he came upon a reason to suspect that she'd been the one to wield the shovel.

Made in the USA
Middletown, DE
08 September 2023

38230831R00142